NATIONAL GALLERY
of ART Washington

NATIONAL GALLERY
of ART Washington

Ross Watson

CRESCENT BOOKS · New York

This edition is published by Crescent Books,
a division of Crown Publishers, Inc.

a b c d e f g h

Printed in Great Britain.

Endpapers: The East Garden Court in the
National Gallery of Art, Washington
Title pages: A view of the West Gallery
from the Mall entrance

PICTURE ACKNOWLEDGMENTS
All illustrations are reproduced by kind permission
of the National Gallery of Art, Washington.
The paintings on the following pages are copyright
S.P.A.D.E.M: 127, 129, 130, 131 and 133.
The painting on page 117 is copyright A.D.A.G.P.

LIBRARY OF CONGRESS CATALOGING IN PUBLICATION DATA

Watson, Ross.
The National Gallery of Art, Washington.

Includes index.
1. United States.   National Gallery of Art.
N856.W38 1979   708'.153   79-335
ISBN 0-517-27168-0

Contents

Foreword

There has been an unprecedented surge of visitors to museums in the last decade, with attendance figures breaking all records with each successive year. More difficult to measure, there seems as well to be a growing number of armchair travelers whose numbers may well be as eager and enthusiastic as the most energetic tourist. This volume will be useful as a companion to both.

The National Gallery of Art has rapidly taken a place as one of the great museums of the world, owing to the generosity of many private donors who have been responsible for the acquisition of every object in the collections. It belongs to the people of the United States who are pleased to share its riches with visitors from all over the world. Opened only since 1941, the Gallery soon became known internationally for the extraordinary holdings of major works by the great masters of Western art. With the opening of the new East Building in June 1978, the scope of activities has broadened to include art of more recent times.

This book is the first to appear since that date and to include examples from our new fields of collecting. It provides a guided tour through a selection of important works of the Gallery's many collections, with detailed information placing each in its appropriate art historical context. It can serve to prepare the prospective viewer for a more productive visit. For the five million and more visitors to the Gallery each year, may it serve as well as a souvenir to remind them of what we hope was a rewarding and enjoyable visit to the National Gallery of Art in Washington.

J. CARTER BROWN
Director, National Gallery of Art,
Washington

Introduction

The National Gallery of Art, Washington, stands at the end of a long line of museums and galleries which span the main cultural centres of Europe and America: Paris, London, Berlin, Madrid, Munich, Leningrad, Vienna, New York, and Boston, Massachusetts, are just some of these. It is the latest, and perhaps the last, of the great palaces devoted to the visual arts in the Western world. Some of these were princely collections, the accumulation, inevitable in ruling families, of court patronage. However, in the United States of America there were no princely or aristocratic collections to form the nucleus of great public galleries. Indeed, until the middle of the nineteenth century there was very little art collecting at all, and there were only a few small museums. The founding of both the Boston Museum of Fine Arts and the Metropolitan Museum, New York, in 1870, must, therefore, have seemed daring ventures. But they soon justified themselves, and by their existence informed public taste and encouraged individuals to collect and to add to the museums' collections. Travelling to Europe became easier, and with it came a greater knowledge of European galleries. Many a well-to-do American merchant or manufacturer returned fired with the resolve that his home town must have an art gallery. Contemporary works, especially those of the Barbizon and Impressionist schools, were admired and collected in the United States at a time when they were ignored or ridiculed in Europe. Thus the United States has, from the beginning, held a commanding position in contemporary art, a position which it has maintained. Sheltered from the effects of two world wars, which have brought political and social revolution to much of Europe, the United States has been able to benefit from the break-up of aristocratic collections as a result of the impoverishment of the owners. A generous tax advantage to American collectors giving works of art to museums has also benefited the public, as the measure provides collectors with every financial incentive to share their treasures with their fellow citizens. Thus, what had been the private pleasure of a few can now be enjoyed by everyone who visits the galleries of a museum.

The lack of a national gallery in the United States had long excited the concern of art lovers. Was the United States to be behind the leading European countries, especially when it prided itself on greater freedom and opportunity? One difficulty lay in the reluctance of Congress to spend public money on the arts at a time when private enterprise was the sacrosanct foundation of the 'American way of life'. The less government interference there was, the better. We have only to look back on Congress's hesitation about accepting James Smithson's bequest in the nineteenth century to understand the obstacles in the way of a national gallery. The cultural life of the United States would indeed have been poorer without the Smithsonian, although it was primarily a scientific and historical institution. At least the Smithsonian, once established, did provide a parent body onto which a future national gallery could be engrafted and, in fact, Congress set up part of the Institution to be the legal depositary for all works of art belonging to the nation. This branch came to be called the National Gallery of Art and is the parent of the present National Collection of Fine Arts. The most important single collection belonged to Harriet Lane Johnston, niece of President Buchanan, who left her pictures to the Corcoran Gallery with the proviso that they were to go to a national gallery in Washington, should one be established. In the case settling the disputed bequest, in 1906, the court decided that such a body already existed as part of the Smithsonian, thus legally confirming its position. The general level of the collections was not above mediocre and in no sense could the then National Gallery be considered a worthy representative. There was a rather strange plan by an architect named Franklin Webster Smith for the National Galleries of History and Art as part of the 'Aggrandizement of Washington'. These ideas were published in 1900 by the Government Printing Office and make curious reading. Smith's idea was anything but modest; he proposed a site of over 62 acres of galleries, courts and avenues in the area of the Old Observatory between 26th and 22nd Streets to the west of the White House. The buildings and courtyards would have been in varying architectural styles from Egyptian to Gothic, with an American Acropolis and Valhalla corresponding to the Capitol on the eastern side of Washington. The cost was estimated at $10,000,000 and, not surprisingly, the scheme was never adopted. What was needed to establish a national gallery was a rich, public-spirited individual who owned a collection of the first importance and would provide a suitable building to contain it. This unlikely combination of desirables was eventually found in Andrew W. Mellon.

Andrew Mellon possessed enormous wealth, his fortune being based on the heavy industries of Pittsburgh. In addition to managing his extensive financial holdings, he served as Secretary of the Treasury under Presidents Harding, Coolidge and Hoover from 1921 to 1932, and was appointed ambassador to Great Britain in 1932. Mellon built up his collection of more than 150 paintings and sculptures over several decades. He had become interested in art through his friend Henry Clay Frick, with whom he used to travel to Europe looking at museums. Doubtless Frick's decision to build a gallery in New York influenced Mellon's thoughts when he came to Washington. Andrew Mellon relied extensively on two major dealers of the day, Knoedler and Duveen, who competed for his patronage. They would bring a painting to his Washington apartment and leave it on his wall for a few months so Mellon could become accustomed to it and decide whether or not to buy. Later, Duveen rented a flat below Mellon's where he displayed paintings and sculpture which were for sale. Mellon bought the important Dreyfus Collection of Renaissance sculpture from Duveen because he felt that, unlike the National Gallery, London, which was his model, his gallery should not be confined to paintings. The most important acquisitions, and certainly the most spectacular, came from the sale of works from the Hermitage Museum by the Russian government. In this way 21 paintings passed to the Mellon Collection. These included two Raphaels, three van Dycks, five Rembrandts, two paintings by Hals, and works by Titian, Botticelli, Perugino and van Eyck. Long before this great coup in 1931 to 1932, it had been Andrew Mellon's determination to provide a national gallery in Washington which would attract additional collections. In December 1936 he wrote to President Franklin Roosevelt offering his collection of paintings and sculpture to the American people together with a capital sum for the building of a gallery. He modestly requested that his own name should not be used in the denomination, although for long the people of Washington referred to the National Gallery of Art as the Mellon Gallery. In his letter Andrew Mellon said: 'Over a period of many years I have been acquiring important and rare paintings and sculpture with the idea that ultimately they would become the property of the people of the United States and be made available to them in a national art gallery . . . Such a gallery would be for the use and benefit of the general public; and it is my hope that it may attract gifts from other citizens who may in the future desire to contribute works of art of the highest quality to form a great national collection . . . I shall stipulate that the proposed building shall not bear my name, but be known as The National Art Gallery or by such other name as may appropriately identify it as a gallery of art of the National Government.'

Andrew Mellon's plan was approved without difficulty in Congress. A joint resolution specified that 'no work of art shall be included in the permanent collection of the National Gallery of Art unless it be of similar high standard of quality to those in the collection acquired from the donor'. A sum of $5,000,000, later increased to $10,000,000, was provided, over and above the cost of erecting the building, for the salaries of the five senior members of the staff and towards future purchases. Although established as a unit of the Smithsonian Institution, the new National Gallery was to have its own board of trustees. These include, *ex officio*, the Chief Justice of the Supreme Court, who is chairman of the board, the Secretary of State, the Secretary of the Treasury and the Secretary of the Smithsonian Institution, together with five other members who have to be private citizens. With the passing of time, the links between the Smithsonian and the National Gallery have become more tenuous and the latter has achieved a semi-autonomous status. Maintenance of the building and the administrative costs were all assumed by the United States government, and in these days of ever rising costs and salaries, the danger of having to reduce essential services, such as having regular opening hours or showing all the exhibition galleries, which some private museums have had to curtail, has been avoided.

Building began in 1937, but unfortunately neither the founder nor the architect, John Russell Pope, were to see their work completed, for both died within 24 hours of each other in August 1937. The National Gallery opened on 17 March 1941. In his speech accepting the National Gallery on behalf of the United States, President Roosevelt referred to the war, then raging in half the world, which would soon involve America's intervention. He reaffirmed the belief of the American people in freedom and democracy. The works of art were 'symbols of the human spirit, and of the world against which armies are now raised and countries overrun and men imprisoned and their work destroyed . . . To accept this work today is to assert the purpose of the people of America that the freedom of the human spirit and human mind which has produced the world's great art and all its science shall not be utterly destroyed . . . The dedication of this Gallery to a living past, and to a greater and more richly living future, is the measure of the earnestness of our intention that the freedom of the human spirit shall go on'. Within eight months the United States confirmed that intention by entering the Second World War.

In 1937 another collection had joined the Mellon gift. Samuel H. Kress, founder of a chain of 'five and ten cent' stores, with branches throughout the United States, gave over 400 paintings and 35 pieces of sculpture, all from the Italian schools, to the National Gallery. These included such masterpieces as Giorgione's *Allendale Adoration,* a panel from Duccio's *Maestà,* a *Madonna* by Giotto and many other works of the highest quality. Kress had the unusual and admirable idea of transferring the profits from his business into paintings and sculpture for the public to enjoy. Later, through the Kress Foundation, in which his brother Rush played a leading part, the collection was extended to include other continental European schools, and eventually numbered about 1500 paintings and pieces of sculpture. Only part of the Kress Collection is exhibited in Washington; the remainder has been dispersed to galleries in towns the length and breadth of the United States, as well as to colleges and universities, thus bringing works of art to the widest possible audience, especially in areas which were not already well provided. It is difficult to single out examples from the great richness of the Kress Collection which the National Gallery received, but among non-Italian paintings outstanding ones are: David's portrait of *Napoleon in his Study,* Ingres' *Madame Moitessier,* four splendid Fragonards, including *Blind Man's Buff* and *The Swing,* Clouet's *'Diane de Poitiers',* a Dürer *Madonna,* an excessively rare Grünewald, *The Small Crucifixion,* and El Greco's *Laocoön.* In Italian painting every school and almost every major artist from the fourteenth to the eighteenth century is represented.

Shortly after the National Gallery's opening a third important collection was given by Joseph E. Widener in memory of his father, Peter A. B. Widener, a railway magnate who had begun acquiring paintings, sculpture and works of art at the turn of the century. Joseph Widener, although he lived in Philadelphia, had already considered building a gallery in Washington to house his collection. When the Widener gift arrived in 1942, it included such masterpieces as Castagno's heroic *David,* Raphael's *Small Cowper Madonna, The Feast of the Gods* by Bellini, an unparalleled array of van Dycks from the artist's Genoese period, Vermeer's *Woman Holding a Balance* and an important group of Rembrandts. The 100 paintings ranging from the Italian *Quattrocento* to Renoir indicate the breadth of the collection, which also includes Italian marbles and bronzes, eighteenth-century French sculpture and works of art ranging from Abbot Suger's chalice to furniture by Riesener.

Hitherto, apart from a few French Impressionists in the Widener collection and isolated gifts, the Gallery's paintings had been confined to the established Old Masters. The great developments in the second half of the nineteenth century and the twentieth century were almost ignored. This gap was filled by the munificent bequest of the financier Chester Dale who, through his wife, Maud, had become interested in French painting and put together one of the most extensive and representative collections in the United States. This included ten paintings by Monet, nine by Renoir, eight by Degas, six by Toulouse Lautrec, six by Cézanne, five by van Gogh, four by Gauguin, eleven Picassos and nine Matisses. For many years before Dale's death in 1962, part of the collection had been on loan to the Gallery. Now the range extended into the twentieth century, almost to the present day – from Delacroix to Picasso and Matisse.

While the main emphasis of the National Gallery of Art has always been on European painting, even at the beginning there were examples from the American school. Andrew Mellon bought a group of portraits, some of which, being of historical interest, were to go to a national portrait gallery should one be established. This is now happily the case and 20 historical portraits have been transferred there. The American paintings then admired were either by artists who had visited Europe or who had been influenced by the European tradition. Changing taste has led to an appreciation of painters working in a native style, inspired by the grandeur of the American landscape or incidents from American life. The primitive painters, who owed little or nothing to 'great art', perhaps give a truer vision, in their naïveté, of America from colonial days until the time of the Civil War. Beginning in 1953, Edgar William Garbisch and his wife Bernice Chrysler Garbisch have donated several hundred primitives so that these important examples of American painting should have a place in its National Gallery of Art.

The National Gallery has no legal or logical 'cut-off' date for acquisitions. Few collections can or would wish to remain static, and today's contemporary painters will become the Old Masters of tomorrow. With the rise in importance of the School of New York, America's first major original contribution to international painting, it makes perfect sense to include works by contemporary artists in the East Building, designed in an unashamedly modern style by I. M. Pei, and opened in 1978. In addition to works of sculpture by Calder and David Smith, *Lavender Mist* by Jackson Pollock, Robert Motherwell's *Reconciliation Elegy,* and other important examples of American paintings have also been acquired. The extensive spaces in the new building are especially appropriate for the huge Matisse collages recently bought by the museum, and for large-scale tapestries.

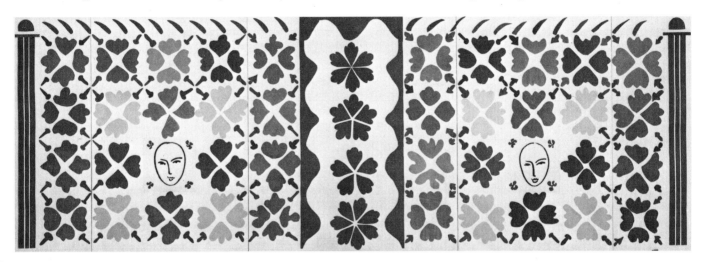

Above: In his last years Matisse confined himself to cut-outs. A group of these is exhibited in a specially-designed gallery in the East Building.

Andrew Mellon's wish that the National Gallery should not be confined to paintings was reflected in his own collection of prime examples of Italian Renaissance sculpture; this was augmented by the Widener gift which also included eighteenth-century French sculpture. Both periods were well covered in the Kress Collection, and the Foundation added the wonderfully rich collection of Renaissance bronzes, reliefs and medals formerly belonging to Gustave Dreyfus, which is one of the finest in the world. Moving forward in time, Mrs John W. Simpson, a friend of Rodin, donated 28 pieces by the sculptor; an extensive collection of Daumier bronzes was presented by Lessing J. Rosenwald; and to mark the opening of the new East Building, a number of examples of contemporary sculpture have been acquired or commissioned, most notably a mobile by Alexander Calder, this sculptor's last work, and *Knife Edge Mirror Two Piece* by Henry Moore. Although neither sculpture nor graphics will be covered in this book, it would be misleading to ignore the important place they hold in the collection. The Print Room is one of the most active sections in the museum and there is hardly a time when it is not holding an exhibition. These exhibitions are often major representations of an artist, or a school, with a detailed catalogue as the permanent record of scholarship. The chief benefactor in both prints and drawings has been Lessing J. Rosenwald, who over a long period has enriched the Print Room with tens of thousands of examples of graphic art from the fourteenth century to the present. Important purchases continue to be made as opportunity allows, thereby building up a representative collection available both for study and research.

The children of the founder, Ailsa Mellon Bruce and Paul Mellon, who is now president of the trustees, have been extremely generous to the National Gallery in gifts of art and money. In addition to bequeathing her collection of nineteenth-and twentieth-century French pictures, Ailsa Mellon Bruce gave funds through which many works of the highest quality have been obtained, most notably Leonardo's portrait of *Ginevra de' Benci,* Georges de la Tour's *The Repentant Magdalen,* Rubens' *Daniel in the Lions' Den* and a splendid series of Matisse collages. The Avalon Foundation, funded by Mrs Bruce, has made possible important acquisitions in American paintings. Mr and Mrs Paul Mellon have given many fine examples of French painting to broaden the Gallery's already rich holdings, and Paul Mellon has presented a very large group of gouache paintings by the American painter George Catlin, who lived with the Indians and made unique records of their life. Both Paul Mellon and Ailsa Mellon Bruce have financed the new East Building which will be discussed later. It would not be possible to list all those generous benefactors who have given works of art to the National Gallery; a brief résumé of the principal donors includes: the W. Averell Harriman Foundation, Ralph and Mary Booth, Governor Alvan T. Fuller, members of the Havemeyer family and Lillian Timken.

While Congress pays for the upkeep and staffing of the National Gallery, no money is provided for acquisitions. This is regarded as something for the private sphere and so the museum has to rely on its own funds for purchases and on the generosity of collectors. Inevitably there will be a certain amount of predatory competition between museums, not only for works which come up at auction or through dealers, but also for the favour of collectors. No museum can afford to ignore potential benefactors,

especially at a time when the cost of paintings has risen so astronomically. Its position as the national gallery of the United States, in the national capital, encourages gifts which the donors feel will be seen by an even wider audience, both American and foreign, than in New York, Boston or Chicago. But the original resolution of Congress, that a 'similar high standard of quality' to that of the Mellon Collection should be maintained, still stands as a guideline. Many works are offered but not accepted, and all potential acquisitions are scrutinized by the curators and have to be approved by the trustees.

The architect, John Russell Pope, was chosen to design the National Gallery of Art; he had already designed the National Archives and the Jefferson Memorial on the Tidal Basin, Washington. Pope provided a dignified and restrained building in pink Tennessee marble which becomes noticeably pinker when wet. The style was classical, as no other would have been considered proper for a public building in Washington, or an art gallery. George Hadfield's City Hall, later the Court House in Washington, built in 1820, provided the basis for the design with its Ionic portico, low central dome and H-shaped ground plan. Now that the Mall (the site on which the gallery stands) has become filled up with other museums and galleries, Pope's building stands out for its essential good taste. It makes no claims

to be great architecture, but it is one of the last to be designed in the tradition of humane rationalism. The large areas of blank wall (the total length of the Gallery is 238 metres) are, for security reasons, without windows, but this is reduced from monotony by blind niches and subtle decorative details. A shallow, saucer dome with stepped base over the centre is the only exception to the flat roof line. An imposing flight of steps leads up to the museum from the Mall, at the top of which, on the main floor, is an octastyle of Ionic columns. There is an alternative approach by lift from Constitution Avenue.

Visitors need information and the National Gallery of Art provides this on various levels. Works of art need to be explained if they are to be appreciated, and for many coming from outside Washington, this will be the first time they will have visited a gallery. On both floors enquiries are answered and plans of the different sections guide visitors to whichever paintings they wish to see. Every day tours of the museum are conducted by members of the Education Department, who are all trained art historians, and they also give a short daily talk on the painting of the week so that over the course of years the whole collection is covered. When there are special exhibitions, which have now become part of the Gallery's normal life, the Education Department is kept busy with group tours, and demand always exceeds supply. To assist the Gallery staff, volunteer lecturers take round parties of school children, and in the spring hundreds of buses line up on the Mall to discharge their passengers at the steps. Guide-books to the permanent collection and catalogues of temporary exhibitions are produced by the Editor's Office and sold through the Publication Department, which does a lively business in postcards and reproductions. To give an overall view of the Gallery an *Annual Report* is published, and curators, visiting fellows and outside scholars contribute to the *Studies in the History of Art*. One day it is hoped to publish a complete scholarly catalogue of the Gallery's holdings, something which all responsible art institutions now regard as an obligation. In the meantime, detailed catalogues have appeared of the Kress Collection and of the Italian paintings.

For groups unable to visit the National Gallery, the Extension Service produces programmes of slides and tapes on a wide variety of subjects based on exhibitions, and these can be borrowed through the mail, free of charge. The service also distributes a multi-media programme with a magazine called *Art and Man* which reaches many thousands of schools. These can also benefit by borrowing from the thousands of renderings in the Index of American Design. The renderings are accurate and beautiful water-colours of American folk objects of the past in glass, earthenware, metal, wood or fabric, ranging from children's samplers to country furniture. They were painted in the Depression under the Federal Art Project to give work to unemployed artists, and are a fascinating record of Americana, often of things now vanished.

Every Sunday afternoon a slide lecture is given in the auditorium, usually by a visiting scholar, on some subject relating to the collection. Each year a scholar of international renown is invited to give the A. W. Mellon lectures, a series of six, which are subsequently published. These have included Kenneth Clark's *The Nude*, E. H. Gombrich's *Art and Illusion* and Jacques Maritain's *Creative Intuition in Art and Poetry*. Kenneth Clark has another link with the National Gallery for his *Civilisation* films were given their first American showing there to enthusiastic audiences. Some who come to listen to the lectures stay on for the Sunday evening concerts in the East Garden Court. The concerts were started during the Second World War when servicemen and their families, looking for somewhere warm, comfortable and free, spent the whole day in the Gallery. There is a resident orchestra, and vocal and instrumental performances are given by artists invited by the conductor, who organizes the music programme. Every year a Festival of American Music provides a chance for music by contemporary composers to be heard, many of the pieces being played for the first time. The fishtail palms and flowers of the East Garden Court, which is matched by a similar one on the west side, are maintained by a horticulturalist and his assistants. There are plants throughout the building which provide a restful relief. At Easter and Christmas the arrays of lilies and poinsettias around the Mercury fountain have become a Washington tradition.

Starting from the majestic Rotunda, with its massive green Italian marble columns, a ceiling inspired by the Pantheon in Rome, and the fountain of Mercury by Adriaen de Vries, which has become a symbol of the National Gallery, two large sculpture halls lead to the East and West Garden Courts. The exhibition galleries are off these halls and courts. These were constructed as the needs of the expanding collection required, and gradually most of the unfinished spaces have been taken over. The paintings are arranged according to schools, and within these are in roughly chronological order, always bearing in mind that great works of art cannot be forced into any preconceived decorative scheme, but must be treated with respect. New methods of lighting, the

Below: The bronze Mercury, *attributed to Adriaen de Vries, stands in a fountain in the Rotunda of the West Building. Mercury's attributes of winged hat and sandals and the statue's central position make it a fitting symbol of the National Gallery's purpose—to bring art to the greatest number of people.*

introduction of varying colours, which provide a lively, almost daring, tone to some of the galleries, and the integration of previously disparate collections, have all, in the last few years, created a more easily comprehensible display and rational arrangement of the paintings. The use of period frames hopes to provide, in some cases at least, the correct setting for a painting, a matter too often ignored in the past, but to which many artists have given considerable thought. Ample seats in the galleries offer relief to the foot-weary visitor, and the Garden Courts offer a peaceful retreat while the café-buffet provides refreshments.

Like any large and complex building, there is a great deal more to running the National Gallery of Art than the public sees or realizes. A large maintenance staff to keep everything in good order is needed: cleaners, painters, carpenters and specialized technicians for heating, cooling and lighting. The fabric of the building must be constantly repaired. For the safety of the paintings, especially those on wood which are more sensitive to environmental fluctuations, temperature and humidity must be set at as constant a level as the variable Washington climate will allow. These levels are checked regularly, as is the amount of light allowed through the glass roof, where special blinds eliminate the damaging effect of ultraviolet rays. All the air coming into the Gallery is filtered to avoid harmful pollution from motor traffic and industrial and domestic fuel oils; this also cuts out dust. In spite of this, there is always dust in the air, so that from time to time picture frames and surfaces have to be carefully wiped clean by curators and members of the conservation staff. Regular inspection by the Registrar's Office ensures that the paintings are kept in good condition and have not suffered any damage. This is difficult to avoid when we consider that in the tourist season

from March to September the galleries are usually very full of tourists, often including school parties eager to see all the sights of Washington in the shortest possible time. In a year, two million visitors come to the National Gallery, either to see the permanent collections, or for one of the increasingly popular exhibitions.

Paintings, like people, need more care as they grow older. When we think of the adventurous history that some of them have had, moving from one country to another or across continents, affected by war and revolution, it is amazing that they have survived so well, some over 700 years. If they are to be enjoyed for further hundreds of years, delicate paintings must be constantly inspected by the Conservation Department, and those in need of first aid, or more serious restoration, must be attended to. Perhaps the separate pieces of a panel are coming apart and the resulting cracks threaten to dislodge the paint; in this case the wood must be stabilized and any surface damage to the paint repaired. Perhaps a canvas has become loose and needs to be stretched, or paint has become dry and is in danger of peeling off. The highly expert conservation staff are also restorers engaged in trying to give a painting as much of its original appearance as possible. Old varnish becomes dark and obscures the colours. Dust makes paintings dirty, and people bring in quantities of it on their clothes and shoes however much the air is filtered. Former restorations change colour at a different rate from the original paint and in time the discrepancy is obvious. Sometimes colour values have altered through chemical processes, but these

Below: X-rays often tell a story about paintings which the surface does not reveal to the naked eye. This painting of Venus started as a portrait; Titian changed his mind, turned the canvas round and began a new work.

are generally irreversible. All these have to be amended by cleaning and touching up. Restorers require great sensitivity as well as technical skill to know how much to do and when to stop; they must somehow try to think themselves into the mind of the original artist in order to understand his creation.

As with the human patient, paintings in the conservation laboratory are now X-rayed. This often provides fascinating information not visible on the surface of a panel or a canvas. The preliminary brushwork, which is sometimes as much a 'signature' of particular artists as their names on the finished painting, can be clearly identified and gives us an insight into their working methods. This can help to decide on the authenticity of paintings, whether they are fakes, or copies, or school pieces; forgeries are quite rare. We can detect the changes, or *pentimenti*, an artist makes and seem to be directly witnessing the creative process. Occasionally, the alterations are radical. Titian's *Venus with a Mirror* was recently discovered to have been painted over the portraits of a man and a woman, and X-rays revealed considerable changes in Venus' clothing and in one of her attendant *putti*. Even more startling are the changes that have become apparent in another of Titian's paintings, or rather one in which he was involved, for it was begun by Giovanni Bellini; this is *The Feast of the Gods*, Bellini's last major painting. Alfonso d'Este, Duke of Ferrara, who had commissioned the painting, became dissatisfied with Bellini's work, which the artist had in any case been reluctant to undertake as the subject matter was uncongenial. The Duke asked Titian to add the more dramatic hilltop on the left, and to unclothe some of the nymphs and goddesses, thereby adding to the erotic element of the painting. The original line of trees, continuing those on the right, can be detected quite clearly on the X-ray, as can the extent of the women's garments which cover their breasts; Bellini had evidently felt this was the seemly manner in which to paint them.

In addition to the practical side of conservation, research has to be carried out on the paints and varnishes used by artists so that their varying properties can be understood. The National Gallery has a research project on artists' materials at the Carnegie-Mellon Institute of Research, Pittsburgh, a pioneer project in the use of science as an aid to art. The findings of these investigations are published. Research into the effects of light and how to prevent colours from fading has also provided valuable information. The difficulty of distinguishing between real and apparent fading was removed by the use of an instrument called a spectrophotometer which enabled colours to be differentiated even when to the eye they appear virtually the same. It was discovered that the fading of colours was conditioned by which white pigment had been used to make up the paint, some greatly accelerating the rate and others much less so. Furthermore, the medium in which a pigment is suspended also affects its rate of fading. These researches have been made available to museums and to conservation experts. Another aspect of the Gallery's research project is to separate the modern forgery from a genuinely old painting. White lead gives off lead and radium through the decay of uranium. This can be measured, and while in its 'natural' state the radioactive emission from all three elements is equal, in the smelted metal the radioactivity of the lead will go down at a precisely measurable rate, while the radium activity is fairly constant. In this way the age of the white lead can be established, and a forgery exposed.

Today, there are few museums which do not put on temporary exhibitions, either from their own reserves or by drawing on outside loans. Certainly it is stimulating to see even familiar paintings in a different context, rather like combining the same ingredients to make a different dish. The ancillary material, whether in the form of decorative objects, pieces of historical interest, blown-up photographs, or explanatory labels, anything which reinforces the theme of the exhibition, underlines particular points the organizers want to make or which helps to clarify something unfamiliar to the public; all this supporting cast has become as important as the principals, so that the latter are in danger, sometimes, of being swamped. The approach, of giving information to the large number of visitors who will be unfamiliar with the subject, is often heavily didactic. It would be interesting to speculate on the reasons for the apparently insatiable appetite of the public for new shows. Society is in a state of constant flux in this television age and soon tires of the familiar, craving for novelty. This is one of the main appeals of advertising whose techniques are being adopted by museums in the struggle for public attention. On a more serious level, there is the opportunity to see inaccessible works of art from distant galleries, which most people could not afford to visit. But the question must be asked if there are not too many exhibitions now in the museum world. Is perhaps the idea being cheapened through excess? More important, are the paintings, usually in a fragile state, being put at risk to satisfy public demand. Every time a work of art travels it is at risk, not only from human carelessness, but from an air disaster, and now there is the frightening possibility of damage from the vandal, the maniac or the terrorist. Accidents do happen, mercifully very rarely, but some day an irreplaceable painting is going to be destroyed and the world's artistic heritage thereby diminished. These are matters which all museum officials have to consider.

The original policy of the National Gallery's trustees was to refuse all loan requests from the permanent collection as these would deplete its still small resources. Later, an exception was made for American paintings. This refusal to lend to other institutions meant that it was difficult to borrow from museums without reciprocal loans. Naturally, this affected the type of exhibition put on at the Gallery in its early years and, for a time, the war cut off any loans from Europe. Some were drawn from its own reserves, like the various anniversary exhibitions showing the Kress acquisitions. Others were collections temporarily homeless, such as the Bliss collection of Pre-Columbian gold, now at Dumbarton Oaks, or Calouste Gulbenkian's paintings, French art and Egyptian sculpture, part of a very rich collection it was hoped might remain permanently at the Gallery, but which went eventually to Lisbon. As a result of the German invasions, paintings from French and Belgian museums and private collections on loan to various exhibitions at the beginning of the Second World War could not return to their home countries and were taken in as refugees. These compensated in some measure for the evacuation of the more important paintings and sculptures from the Gallery after Pearl Harbor. The problem had already been foreseen and a safe refuge found at Biltmore, near Asheville, North Carolina, the palatial Vanderbilt mansion in the French Renaissance style. The war years imposed extra burdens on the Gallery staff, necessarily depleted because of the dispersal of the collections, but for countless thousands of servicemen and women the paintings must have been a refreshing contrast to the outside world, speaking of a higher life than the destruction and horror of war. There were the inevitable showings of patriotic and national art to boost morale. And as an unexpected bonus, some of the great masterpieces from the Kaiser Friedrich Museum in Berlin, which had been discovered by the American army in a salt mine

at the end of the war, were enjoyed by many in Washington and other cities in the United States before going back to Germany. At least something was done in the National Gallery to palliate the destruction and loss of art through the fighting. It became the headquarters of the American Commission for the Protection and Salvage of Artistic and Historic Monuments in War Areas. This commission was concerned both with the recovery of property stolen by the Axis governments and with art endangered by Allied bombing and invasion.

After the war, once normal relations had been resumed between countries, exhibitions of art from Japan, Korea, Taiwan, France, Peru, Colombia and Egypt were held, organized in co-operation with the governments of those countries. In 1949 the wonderful riches of the Vienna collections were temporarily homeless, as the museums that had housed them were being repaired, having sustained damage during the war, and a selection was sent on tour to the United States, beginning in Washington. Its official position as a branch of government and the ability to use the help of the State Department has been very beneficial to the National Gallery in the often delicate negotiations which precede any important foreign loan. At the same time, the Gallery is frequently included on the itinerary of visiting heads of state and government. Two individual works of art, both of the highest importance and among the best-known to the general public, were exhibited by the Italian and French governments. One was Michelangelo's *David*, from the Bargello

in Florence, sent over to America in 1949 and the other was the *Mona Lisa* which received the treatment more generally reserved for Hollywood stars of the first magnitude, when it came to Washington in 1963. Both are examples of the rather questionable alliance of art and high level diplomacy which has shown no signs of abatement in recent years. To celebrate the twenty-fifth anniversary of the opening, a selection of nineteenth- and twentieth-century French paintings from the collections of Mr and Mrs Paul Mellon and Mrs Mellon Bruce was shown in 1966. Many of these paintings, those from Mrs Bruce's collection, were later to join the Gallery permanently.

The tempo of exhibitions has greatly increased since about 1970 and the original lending restriction is no longer in operation. A full-time team of designers is now kept busy providing the settings for shows which are often staged concurrently. The public has come to expect that an exhibition's presentation should be carefully thought out so that the works of art achieve maximum impact. Problems of crowd capacity and circulation have to be foreseen and resolved, frequently in inflexible spaces not designed for the purpose. To mention all the exhibitions shown at the National Gallery of Art in the last decade would be impossible, only the outstanding ones can be listed. Eskimo culture formed the theme of *The Far North*, and there have been two shows devoted to African art which, given the large black population in Washington, were understandably popular. *The Archaeological Finds of the People's Republic of China*, and the *Treasures of Tutankhamun*, shown in various European countries before coming to Washington, in 1974 and 1976 respectively, attracted record-breaking crowds. Public excitement can be gauged by the long queues which stood for hours to see the exhibitions, often in chilly weather, and the Gallery's resources were stretched to the limit during these hectic months. Also very popular were selections from museums in Leningrad and Moscow which were exhibited in two parts, one consisting of French Impressionists and Post-Impressionists, and the other of Old Masters and Russian paintings. These cultural exchanges are part of the friendlier relations between the United States and the Soviet Union. To celebrate the Bicentenary of the American Revolution there were two important loan exhibitions with works borrowed from many countries. The earlier show, actually opening in 1975, was an imaginative evocation of *The European Vision of America*. The second, *The Eye of Thomas Jefferson*, charted the aesthetic odyssey of this many-sided statesman. It was the most elaborate exhibition ever mounted in the National Gallery, and fittingly was preceded by a spectacular display of fireworks at the foot of Capitol Hill. The opening of the East Building in 1978 was marked by a selection from the superb former royal collections in Dresden, which the German Democratic Republic agreed to lend. Keeping a balance between providing the stimulus of new fare for the public and the prime curatorial responsibilities to the permanent collections is always a difficult matter. The new East Building will provide proper exhibition space leaving the galleries in the main building undisturbed.

Because of its extensive wall space the Gallery has not been affected much by the problem which many older institutions face of how to show the reserve collection not on permanent display. The number of paintings kept in storage, not in the basement of popular myth, is small, and thanks to the National Lending Collection, those not required for the Gallery's own use can be borrowed by other museums in the United States, thus finding an appreciative temporary home. In this way art, which might remain out of public sight, will be enjoyed by fresh audiences.

When Congress allocated the site on the Mall for the National Gallery, space was left on the eastern side for future use. In the first years such a need must have seemed almost incredible as ample room still existed in the building. But as the collection grew, the unused space was converted into galleries. Furthermore, a larger curatorial staff, a more complicated administration and the diversified services offered by the National Gallery created the need for more and more offices. No institution is immune from Parkinson's Law, especially with the seemingly inevitable expansion of bureaucracy. With the accelerated exhibitions programme it became unavoidable that some galleries had to be dismantled for a period or permanently. This unsatisfactory state of affairs could not go on, and in 1968 Paul Mellon and his sister Ailsa Mellon Bruce announced that they would finance an extension on the vacant plot – the new East Building. This extension of the National Gallery of Art is in reality a self-contained multi-purpose building. It will provide offices for much of the staff, house a centre for art historians, allow space for temporary exhibitions and, finally, give an appropriate setting for the works of modern painting and sculpture that the Gallery has been acquiring over the last few years. Connecting the two buildings is a granite-paved plaza set about with trees and shrubs. The most eye-catching objects in it are the seven skylights of silvered glass in the form of tetrahedrons. A line of 24 jets forms a fountain and the water falls down a steep slope at the side in the manner of a Persian fountain. The sight and sound of the waterfall can be enjoyed by those using the café-buffet below, to which the tetrahedrons serve as skylights. This replaces the

cafeteria in the West Building with a more modern type of service, the buffet catering for those who want a quick meal, while the café serves those who wish to eat in a more leisurely fashion and enjoy a glass of wine in the style of a European pavement restaurant. They are part of the connecting link between the two buildings, first used in 1976, which exists at several levels and contains mainly offices and workshops. There is, in addition, a loading dock near the Registrar's office where arrivals and departures of works of art can be supervised. A large underground car park for the staff has also been provided. From the Concourse, below the plaza, where next to the café-buffet a new publications sales desk has been set up, a moving walkway gives an alternative means of reaching the East Building in cold or wet weather.

The long tradition of Neoclassical architecture for official buildings in Washington has now come to an end. While the Mall, connecting the Capitol with the Washington Monument, is a sensitive area, the circular Hirshhorn Museum, opened in 1974, had established a precedent for building in a contemporary style. L'Enfant, who planned the city of Washington, provided a series of broad avenues on the diagonals to link up important points and to break the monotony of the grid system. Where an avenue joins a street the corner site will be irregular; this is the case where Pennsylvania Avenue meets the Mall. Its position on the ceremonial route between the White House and the Capitol, the *via triumphalis* of Washington, called for a structure that must satisfy several requirements. It must make an architectural statement of significance, yet must not compete with the Capitol. The classical architecture of the Federal Triangle, and especially of the existing National Gallery building, would have to be respected, and there were height restrictions that had to be observed. The Chinese-American architect I. M. Pei used the challenge of the awkward wedge-shaped site to create an ingenious design. Pei divided the available building ground area, which is a trapezium of over 55,000 square metres, into two triangles by means of a diagonal. The larger triangle, which is isosceles, became the exhibition space, while the smaller, right-angled triangle houses the curatorial and administrative offices and the International Centre for Advanced Study in the Visual Arts. Using the isosceles triangle as a module, the architect has created a variety of spaces for the many purposes of the building and the triangle is repeated in the floors, the skylights and other details. Both the old and new buildings have been kept on the same axis by extending the bisecting line of the Gallery through the plaza until it hits the apex of the larger triangle in the East Building. The line also runs through the two entrances on either side of the plaza, and this, together with the adoption of the same pink Tennessee marble as in the West Building, unites the two parts formally and visually.

The visitor's point of departure, if he is arriving at ground level, is the monumental East door of the Gallery, hitherto seldom used, which has been made into a new entrance on to the plaza and is the link between the two buildings. At the corners of the exhibition section are three massive towers in the shape of parallelograms, again repeating the module of their parent, this time doubled and placed back to back. Apart from a Henry Moore sculpture at the entrance, there is little art outside; the walls have been left plain, the surfaces relying on the quality of the marble and the precision of the unusual angles for their effect. The H-shaped façade facing the plaza has two of these towers rising starkly, and they give a strong vertical accent to counteract the horizontal of the lintel over the entrance. A low-ceilinged lobby has been kept to a minimum height so that the fullest dramatic effect can be gained from the extensive open space of the central court. This rises the full height of the building, 24 metres from the Concourse level through four floors. The steel, aluminium and glass roof composed of tetrahedrons, although 500 tons in weight, gives no feeling of discomfort or oppressiveness. The huge Calder mobile which fills the void as its various parts rotate, seems to float so effortlessly, that it is hard to realize that the largest wing measures four metres across. The court is the core of the exhibition building, and from it all the different levels, Concourse, Lower, Mezzanine and Upper can be seen at once. These changing aperçus and the dramatic staircase give the feeling of a Baroque theatre set or of a Piranesi etching. As there are large expanses of glass, the same materials have been used inside as on the outside walls so that there is a feeling of cohesion without any visual barrier between the two. The diamond-shaped columns and the horizontal members are composed of a special concrete containing marble which tones with its surroundings. Their surfaces have a subtle pattern of parallel lines formed from the imprint of the moulds, negative impressions, as it were, of wood. Large shrubs in planters carry the foilage of the Mall into the building and break down the division between it and the surroundings. Light pours in from the roof and from side windows, even percolating to the areas below ground level. A few large-sized works of art are shown in the central court where they fit in with the scale, but the main galleries are in the towers on various levels, and here the growing collection of contemporary art will be displayed, as well as works on loan. On the north side, on Pennsylvania Avenue, there is a sculpture pool. Sculpture will also be exhibited on a site west of the main building which has been laid out in co-operation with the National Park Service. Here, a circular pool has been made, which, in winter, is used by skaters. The exhibition spaces are left flexible with movable walls and adjustable ceilings so that the right scale can be provided, depending on the size and number of works to be shown. The Concourse galleries will be the new site for temporary shows, again allowing for the greatest flexibility in design; this floor has two auditoriums catering for different sized audiences. A terrace café, overlooking the Mall, provides the East Building with its own refreshment facilities.

In 1967 the idea of establishing a study centre was first seriously investigated. Washington has a great deal to offer as a potential centre; firstly, the riches and variety of its collections: the National Gallery itself; the Freer Gallery of Oriental Art; Dumbarton Oaks for Byzantine and Pre-Columbian art; the Phillips Collection with its nineteenth- and twentieth-century art; the Corcoran Gallery; the Hirshhorn Museum for modern art; and the other branches of the Smithsonian. All these give first-hand material of top quality for research. In addition, libraries offering the essential tools of scholarship are abundant, not only with the overall coverage of the Library of Congress, but also specialized libraries in various branches of the arts. At the same time it became apparent that there was a need in the academic world for scholars, both mature professors and those just starting their careers, to find time outside the demands of teaching and administration to prepare original work for publication. Thanks to the generosity of various foundations, the National Gallery has already had a programme of fellowships for graduate students working towards their doctorates. These fellows usually spend part of their time at the Gallery where they can learn about museum life, the remainder of their tenure being allotted to travel abroad. Supervising the fellows is the Kress Professor in

Residence, who is an art historian of eminence, American or European, and usually at the point of retirement from a museum or university post. The new study centre would consequently expand an existing organization and make it more available to scholars at different stages in their careers. They would have the advantage of studying a major art collection at close quarters and the Gallery would benefit from their knowledge and expertise. The present fellowships give a grant of from one to three years and the Kress Professor is appointed annually, but future mature scholars might require a shorter period only for their 'sabbatical', thus allowing more people to benefit from the scheme.

The southern triangle, with its base fronting on to the Mall, houses the Gallery's curatorial and administrative offices as well as the research centre. In contrast to the exhibition segment, the surfaces of the Study Centre are fitted with glass. The broad end of the triangle, facing Capitol Hill, is taken up with six tiers of windows, and there are generous proportions of glass in the other walls. The entrance on the plaza side is reached through a chasm between one of the towers and the sharp point of the triangle rising up like a ship's prow. At the heart, overlooked by the curators' and fellows' offices, is the library, with the main reading room running through six floors. It is filled with light from a full length window giving a view of the Capitol. In the past few years the existing library has been reorganized and expanded, and it is hoped that, through the use of computers, its resources will be of service both nationally and internationally to art historians. Resident scholars will, of course, take advantage of the easy access to such a comprehensive collection. The books are stored on nine levels of stacks with a capacity of 350,000 volumes. Immediately below the library are the photograph archives, another essential aid to art scholarship. In 1945 the National Gallery acquired the Richter Archive, and through the Kress Foundation a systematic programme of purchasing from photographic firms, auction houses and other libraries has multiplied the holdings. Eventually the storage space will accommodate 2,500,000 photographs so that the National Gallery will possess one of the world's major archives. The present slide library will also be enlarged for use in lectures and seminars, as well as being borrowed by art historians outside the Gallery.

There is no doubt that once the business of transferring the library, photo archives and offices to their new quarters has been completed, the East Building will enhance the efficiency of the National Gallery, both through its staff and the services offered to the public. Furthermore, the space relinquished in the main building, which includes almost all the ground floor, can be used for different purposes. Already, the conservation laboratory with the latest technical equipment, has been installed in its new quarters. The complex of offices and galleries will have to be reconstructed and it will take several years for the necessary funding to be available. There are plans to use the Seventh Street entrance exclusively for children and have a reception room, a special room for their activities and a children's museum. More space might be given to the Prints and Drawings Department for exhibitions, the Kress small-scale bronzes, medallions and plaques might once more be displayed, and the decorative arts could then return to the Widener rooms specially created for them. Whatever improvements are made, they will certainly increase the convenience of the main building and give the public access to an even larger area than at present. They demonstrate that the National Gallery of Art is a constantly developing institution ready to adapt to changing needs, while keeping the high standards required to maintain a great collection.

1 DUCCIO DI BUONINSEGNA
The Calling of the Apostles Peter and Andrew
Wood, 43.5 × 46 cm
Samuel H. Kress Collection

DUCCIO DI BUONINSEGNA
Siena active 1278 – 1318/19
The Calling of the Apostles Peter and Andrew
Plate 1

The classical tradition of the Graeco-Roman world, emphasizing the importance of man and humanistic activities, survived in the Byzantine empire centred on Constantinople. However, this eastern Roman empire had become Christian and at times the emphasis on the spiritual, which religious art required, introduced a deliberate irrationality which ran counter to the tradition of realism and naturalism achieved by classical civilization. Mosaics and ikons are essentially two dimensional, relying for their effect on the decorative arrangements of colour and pattern. Byzantine painters were not interested in depicting the weight and volume of figures, nor in creating a rational space around them as can be seen from their mosaics and ikons. Italy, which long remained part of the Byzantine world, felt this influence strongly, and with the revival of painting in the thirteenth century, the Byzantine style was naturally predominant. It took time for artists to emancipate themselves from what had once been a vigorous style, but which was now often only a schematic formula. The vitality of the medieval Italian city states, based on economic prosperity, can be seen in the strong feeling of independence, each jealously watching its neighbour and engaged in endless disputes. They took great pride in their public buildings and the art adorning them. When in 1311 Duccio completed the *Maestà,* or Virgin in Majesty, of which this panel and another in the National Gallery are parts, the citizens of Siena carried the painting in triumph through the streets to the cathedral. Duccio's masterpiece still shows a strong Byzantine influence, but already there is a move away from the static quality of the ikon and a definite attempt to introduce a more natural style. While the landscape background to Christ is still formalized and makes no attempt at correct recession, the three figures are solidly constructed. We can feel the weight of the heavy net as the Apostles stand interrupted at their fishing. The psychological link is underlined by the outstretched hands and the meeting glances of Jesus and Peter as the fishermen listen hesitatingly to Christ's summons.

GIOTTO
Colle di Vespignano c 1267 – Florence 1337
Madonna and Child
Plate 2

With Giotto, the Florentine school established its primacy in Italian painting. No longer looking back to the Byzantine tradition, painters and sculptors developed a new monumentality through giving us the feeling of solidity in their figures and creating a credible space for them to inhabit. This was all the result of a renewed interest in the Roman past, remains of which were everywhere. At the same time, French Gothic art introduced a new emotion and elegance into painting. These two influences can be seen in Giotto's *Madonna*. The firmly modelled features and bold outline, the robust Child sitting in the Virgin's arm,

which really does bear his weight, and the folds of the robe, not merely calligraphic lines but following the contours of the body: all these are evidence of the new naturalism in his style. The touching gesture of the Christ child holding one of his mother's fingers while he reaches for the rose, a symbol of the Passion, in her hand, introduces a tenderness hitherto lacking. The gold background still denies any feeling of dimension, but this is a visionary image of the Queen of Heaven, which must have been impressive when the tooled details of the haloes and the once bright blue robe caught the candlelight in a dark church.

FRA ANGELICO and FRA FILIPPO LIPPI
Vicchio di Mugello 1387 – Rome 1455, Florence c 1406 – Spoleto 1469
The Adoration of the Magi
Plate 3

This magnificent example of fifteenth-century Florentine painting, one of the greatest masterpieces to survive, is a source of endless fascination in the many details of the Three Kings and their train. The painting, which may have belonged to Lorenzo de' Medici, was probably begun by Fra Angelico, who painted the Madonna and Child, and perhaps set the general outline of the composition. His work was interrupted when he went to Rome around 1446. Later, Fra Filippo Lippi completed the painting and most of the figures and some of the background are from his hand. There appear to be at least three distinct styles in the painting which some scholars attribute to the intervention of a pupil of Fra Filippo, others to his having worked on two separate occasions. It has also been argued that the entire work is the responsibility of Fra Filippo Lippi alone.

The worship of the infant Christ by the Magi provided a subject with ample scope for exotic and colourful scenes, and the brilliant reds, blues and yellows of the costumes create a wonderfully joyous atmosphere. This is reinforced by the gilded

haloes and accessories of the main figures, and in the tapestry-like foreground covered with flowers. Compositionally, the painters were not concerned about recreating a scientific space with correctly receding orthogonals, but rather in creating a decorative background. Thus the circular form, particularly popular in Florence, is echoed in the two groups of spectators following the rim of the painting, and the central hills, with their peculiar rock formation, make little attempt to recede naturally. The interior of the stable appears to be like some mine going into the hillside, although it is clearly intended to be in front. Scattered throughout are symbolic references which have often become obscure over the centuries, but contemporaries would have understood them. The peacock and pheasant on the roof symbolize immortality and hope, appropriate to the infant Christ and the message of redemption and salvation he brings to mankind.

FRA FILIPPO LIPPI
Madonna and Child
Plate 4

Devotion to the Virgin Mary was universal in medieval Europe. She was venerated as the chief intercessor between God and man, and nearly every church had an altar dedicated to her. Unlike the still hieratic images of the previous century, Fra Filippo Lippi's Virgin is very much a human mother. She is no longer a celestial being to be worshipped, and while it would be a mistake to regard this as less spiritual because of its greater human value, undoubtedly the barrier between heaven and earth has been removed. What could be more natural than the charming gesture of the Child, one hand holding his mother's while he grasps a finger with the other? Yet there is an introspective quality in the melancholy sweetness of the Virgin, and the Child broods, as if both are thinking of the pain and suffering that lie ahead. Gone is

the gold background in the Byzantine tradition and instead we have a niche with a fluted top in the most advanced classical manner. It might have been a niche for a Donatello statue or an architectural detail in a Brunelleschi building. Lippi was well aware of the advances being made in the other visual arts. At the same time, the background gives a satisfactory formal setting for the figures. The niche also defines them in space, giving them a three dimensional reality. In this Filippo Lippi follows the example of his master Masaccio.

Above
3 FRA ANGELICO AND FRA FILIPPO LIPPI
The Adoration of the Magi
Wood, Diameter 137.2 cm
Samuel H. Kress Collection

Right
4 FRA FILIPPO LIPPI
Madonna and Child
Wood, 80 × 51 cm
Samuel H. Kress Collection

ANDREA DEL CASTAGNO
Castagno c 1420 – Florence 1457
Portrait of a Man
Plate 5

While Masaccio was the most influential painter in the formation of Castagno's style, he turned equally to Donatello's sculpture for inspiration. In the tandem advances of the sister arts one frequently made more rapid progress than the other. So it was in the second quarter of the fifteenth century, when the sculpture busts of Donatello achieved a greater realism than did paintings. We can easily imagine Castagno's portrait in marble or bronze, and the almost metallic forms of the drapery and the hard face, as if made of stone, confirm this. Each form is outlined to give it more distinctness, and the clear contours of the head and shoulders, standing sharply against the sky, are still two dimensional in feeling. It is a powerful portrait, but unlike his Flemish contemporaries, Castagno makes little attempt to model the forms through light and shadow. Everything is seen with the clarity of the strong Italian sunlight, but without any of the atmospheric subtleties to soften the transition from one part to another. We do not know for certain the young man's identity; he may have been a soldier belonging to a noble family, rather than one of the patrician bankers who ruled Florence at the time. His unfaltering gaze and stern expression, so aptly matched in the painting style, would certainly be appropriate for a military leader.

GIOVANNI DI PAOLO
Siena c 1400 – 1482
The Adoration of the Magi
Plate 6

Protected by its hills from Florentine invasion, Siena paid the price of political independence by becoming a cultural backwater from the late fourteenth century. Beautiful paintings were still produced, but the mainstream had moved elsewhere and the great advances in realism through perspective, light, and form took place in Florence. The old-fashioned usages lingered on, as here, in the Byzantine tradition of a cave rather than a stable for the birthplace of Christ. Duccio had used the same motif in a *Nativity*, painted over a hundred years before, which is also in the National Gallery. The figures have been spaced decoratively across the composition like a frieze without any attempt at depth. The painter has concentrated on the elegance of the figures, their stylish clothes and hair, in keeping with the courtly scene of the Virgin and Child receiving the Kings' homage. The background, with carefully cultivated fields, and dotted with fruit trees is recognizably a Tuscan landscape. But although Giovanni di Paolo has tried to preserve a common vanishing point on the left, where the incised lines are carefully drawn, he has made no such attempt on the right, and the building has several different viewpoints. The panel is part of a predella, which is the series of small paintings at the bottom of an altarpiece illustrating the lives of the saints represented in the main panel, or incidents from the life of Christ.

DOMENICO VENEZIANO
died Florence 1461
Saint John in the Desert
Plate 7

Domenico Veneziano may, as his name suggests, have been Venetian by birth, but he was certainly a Florentine painter. He was particularly interested in colour changes through light, which his even greater pupil Piero della Francesca explored in greater depth. Paintings by Domenico are extremely rare, so the Gallery is very fortunate in possessing three, a *Madonna and Child,* and *Saint Francis Receiving the Stigmata,* which is, like the *Saint John,* part of an altarpiece now dispersed in various museums. The main panel was painted for a church of Saint Lucy in Florence about 1450, and is one of the earliest examples of a *sacra conversazione*, or grouping of the Madonna and Child with Saints, where the figures are united thematically instead of being separated into the different panels of a polyptych. In spite of the small scale of this predella painting, the figure has a heroic quality like a Greek athlete or a Hercules as he wraps the goat skin around his shoulders. Saint John, leaning forward to discard his worldly clothes, achieves perfect equilibrium in his body. Perhaps Domenico was influenced by antique sculpture. Certainly the young saint could have been a Renaissance bronze. His difficult choice between the ties of the material world and his higher duty provides an emotional tension, heightened by the jagged mountains in the background which are symbolic of the hard life in the desert.

Left
5 ANDREA DEL CASTAGNO
Portrait of a Man
Wood, 54 × 40.5 cm
Andrew W. Mellon Collection

Below
6 GIOVANNI DI PAOLO
The Adoration of the Magi
Wood, 26 × 45 cm
Andrew W. Mellon Collection

7 DOMENICO VENEZIANO
Saint John in the Desert
Wood, 28.4 × 32.4 cm
Samuel H. Kress Collection

8 STYLE OF ANDREA DEL VERROCCHIO (POSSIBLY LEONARDO)
Madonna and Child with a Pomegranate
Wood, 15.7 × 12.8 cm
Samuel H. Kress Collection

STYLE OF ANDREA DEL VERROCCHIO (POSSIBLY LEONARDO)
Fifteenth-century Florentine
Madonna and Child with a Pomegranate
Plate 8

Many promising young artists worked in the studio of the painter, sculptor and goldsmith Verrocchio. The most distinguished was Leonardo da Vinci. The *Madonna and Child* is undoubtedly from the Verrocchio circle because of a resemblance to his work, but there are also similarities to early Madonnas by Leonardo, which is why some scholars have attributed the painting to him. The beautiful landscape, obviously based on Tuscan views, is worthy of Leonardo, who made many detailed landscape studies, both real and imaginary. If the size were not known, the painting could be mistaken for one much larger; even on this small scale there is none of the fussiness of a miniature such as found in contemporary illuminated manuscripts. The composition is simple: basically the figures form a triangle, the Madonna's head is set against a dark wall, providing the ancient attribute of royalty (the cloth of honour) with a window on either side. The golden highlights of her hair and veil are picked out in gold. With lowered eyelids the Virgin looks down at the seeds of the pomegranate which is a symbol of the Passion.

Left
9 FILIPPINO LIPPI
Portrait of a Youth
Wood, 51 × 35.5 cm
Andrew W. Mellon Collection

Below
10 SANDRO BOTTICELLI
The Adoration of the Magi
Wood, 70.2 × 104.2 cm
Andrew W. Mellon Collection

FILIPPINO LIPPI
Florence c 1457 – 1504
Portrait of a Youth
Plate 9

Painters, like medieval craftsmen, often handed down workshops to their children and the workshops were frequently family enterprises. It could not be guaranteed that talent could also be inherited, but surprisingly enough, there were many dynasties of painters. Filippino Lippi, the son of a nun Filippo Lippi had abducted, was a worthy successor to his father, with whom he began his painting career. He later worked in Botticelli's studio and the influence of his master can be seen in this portrait. Indeed, at one time the painting was attributed to Botticelli. The almost frontal pose gives force to the young man's gaze as he stares directly at us. His head stands out sharply against the pale blue sky which reinforces the strong red of his hat. A cool even light bathes the face. There are shadows, but the stippled brush strokes of egg tempera do not allow the subtle gradations between highlight and shadow which were being achieved by Flemish painters at this time through the use of oil.

SANDRO BOTTICELLI
Florence 1445 – 1510
The Adoration of the Magi
Plate 10

Botticelli is one of the best loved artists of the Florentine Renaissance, and he held a special appeal for the Victorians. There can be few who do not know his *Primavera* or the *Birth of Venus* both of which are in Florence. He painted several Adorations, the subject no doubt attracting him for the opportunities it gave for narrative, in which he excelled. The composition divides easily into three sections in the manner of earlier tryptics, the columns marking the divisions and keeping the central figures as a distinct group from the two semicircles of worshippers on either side. Perhaps because the picture was painted in Rome, Botticelli chose to represent the ruins, symbolizing the Synagogue of the Old Testament which Christ came to replace, in the form of a ruined classical building, which also serves as the traditional stable. Some of the faces look like portraits, possibly, as was frequently the case, of those who commissioned the painting. We can see a few of Botticelli's mannerisms, which later were to become exaggerated, in the elongated body of the Virgin and in the twisting figures inclining towards the centre with their heads tilted to one side. Here they add to the warmth and excitement of the worshippers. Particularly beautiful is the group of horsemen on the right, one of them holding a rearing horse, perhaps based on a famous classical sculpture called the *Dioscuri*, which was in Rome.

BENOZZO GOZZOLI
Florence c 1421 – Pistoia 1497
The Dance of Salome
Plate 11

One of the best known works in Florence, which every visitor must have seen, is Gozzoli's *Procession of the Magi* in the Medici Palace. Art historians may dismiss it as too obviously charming and outside the advanced stream of Florentine painting, but the frescoes remain perennial favourites and it is difficult not to succumb to Gozzoli's appeal. His delight in the things of this world, so unlike the spiritual atmosphere of his master Fra Angelico, is apparent in this predella panel, part of a now dismembered altarpiece. Saint John the Baptist was the leading patron of Florence and for that reason appears frequently in art. The painting shows three different episodes of his martyrdom as if they were taking place at the same time. On the right, Salome dances for her step-father Herod, who is in love with her. The dance is supposed to have been very voluptuous, but we would not guess this from the decorous movements of the young girl, whose clothing would satisfy the demands of the most rigorous prude. The king was so delighted with her performance that he granted Salome anything she wanted and, prompted by her mother, she asked for John's head. On the left, the Baptist's execution is depicted, and in the central background his head is presented to Herodias (Herod's wife), who was thus revenged for the saint's denunciation of her private life. Gozzoli has been careful to create a unified perspective through the beams of the ceiling, and he gives Corinthian pilasters to Herod's banqueting hall, but in spite of this awareness of contemporary developments he is content to follow Gothic tradition in the illogical tripartite composition, the decorative arrangement of his figures and their elegant, unclassical proportions.

11 BENOZZO GOZZOLI
The Dance of Salome
Wood, 23.8 × 34.3 cm
Samuel H. Kress Collection

PIERO DI COSIMO
Florence c 1462 – c 1521
The Visitation with Saint Nicholas and Saint Anthony Abbot
Plate 12

This painting is a variation on the popular *sacra conversazione* where the Madonna and Child are shown with groups of saints. Saint Nicholas, the patron of children, was a fourth century bishop in Asia Minor. Neither he, nor Saint Anthony, a third century hermit who founded monasticism in Egypt, were of course present at the Visitation. They are here to meditate on the great mystery taking place behind them. The Virgin greets her cousin Elizabeth who will soon give birth to John the Baptist. The older woman raises her hand to bless the Virgin for the child Jesus that she will bear. With their identifying attributes – three golden balls for Saint Nicholas, and the crutch, bell and pig of Saint Anthony – the two foreground figures are like heraldic supporters to the central drama. Almost sculptural in their massiveness, the seated men balance each other. So also do the two women, whose deep emotion is expressed by the hand clasp and their intense gaze into each other's eyes. In the background are other scenes connected with Christ's birth: a painting on the church, of the Annunciation, the Adoration of the Shepherds, the Procession of the Magi and the Massacre of the Innocents. These are all related to the main theme and unite the fanciful landscape setting with the foreground figures.

12 PIERO DI COSIMO
The Visitation with Saint Nicholas and Saint Anthony Abbot
Wood, 184 × 189 cm
Samuel H. Kress Collection

GIOVANNI BELLINI
Venice c 1430 – 1516
The Feast of the Gods
Plate 13

Bellini for many years dominated the artistic world in Venice, and during his long career Venetian painting moved from the hard, dry style of the Vivarini to the mellow tones and warm colours so closely associated with that school. Bellini himself came under the influence of many painters, mainly his brother-in-law Mantegna and later, the Sicilian Antonello da Messina, who, if he did not introduce the technique of Flemish oil painting, certainly began a new style in portraits and altarpieces. We associate Bellini chiefly with religious works, especially his series of Madonnas. He was therefore ill suited to carry out the commission of Alfonso d' Este, Duke of Ferrara,

who wished to have a painting from the distinguished Venetian, then at the close of his life, for his study, which was to be decorated with a series of mythological paintings. The subject of Bellini's contribution is drawn from Ovid's *Fasti*: the story of Priapus, the god of fertility. At the moment depicted, the feasting gods, together with nymphs and satyrs, are watching Priapus attempting to make love to the sleeping nymph Lotis. His amatory advances are prevented by the braying of Silenus' ass, which wakes Lotis, who then escapes. The ass can be seen on the left of the composition about to bray. Bellini was unwilling to undertake the commission and treated the subject with the greatest

13 GIOVANNI BELLINI
The Feast of the Gods
Canvas, 170 × 185 cm
Widener Collection

decorum. No one would be aware that anything lascivious is taking place, and the spectators only betray a mild interest in the drama. It is a beautiful painting, but static.

Duke Alfonso became dissatisfied with the picture as it did not fit in with the works he later commissioned from Titian. In the meanwhile, Bellini had died, two years after completing *The Feast*, so the Duke asked Titian, who had already assisted Bellini on the painting, to make alterations. These changes are clearly revealed in the X-rays which show where the clothes of the nymphs and goddesses were lowered to expose their breasts, making the erotic atmosphere more explicit. At the same time, a belt of trees on the left, continuing those on the right side, was

replaced by the more dramatic craggy hill. The alterations certainly give a more convincing appearance to the subject, and make the composition livelier. Duke Alfonso was satisfied that the painting would now harmonize with the other decorations of bacchanals in his study. The story is a fascinating example of the power of a patron's wishes during the Renaissance.

The three dishes shown conspicuously in the central portion of the picture are Ming, and must be among the earliest representations of Chinese porcelain in western painting.

CARLO CRIVELLI
Venice c 1430 – Ascoli Piceno c 1493
Madonna and Child Enthroned with Donor
Plate 14

It has been the fate of many altarpieces to be broken up and their various parts dispersed among different collections. Three subsidiary sections of this central panel are in other American museums and another is in the National Gallery, London. Crivelli had a very distinctive style, the result of his admiration for Mantegna, combined with a mannered Late Gothic tradition. The flesh of his figures has the texture and colour of parchment; the fingers are long and bone-like and he draws a hard line around objects. Everything is painted with great clarity, and each object is treated with equal importance, leading to a lack of atmospheric feeling. Crivelli's sad and wistful Madonna still retains something of the ikon, deriving from Venice's Byzantine heritage, and the composition is full of decorative details which also have a symbolic meaning. The strange dolphin arms to the throne and similar dolphins above the niche refer to the belief that they transported the souls of the dead; they consequently symbolize resurrection and salvation. The apples represent original sin, which Christ, holding one in his hand, will overcome, while the pears refer to his love for mankind. By about 1490, when this altarpiece was painted, the use of gold had come to be considered old fashioned, for it denied the illusion of space. In the same way, the medieval tradition of showing the donor on a smaller scale had been discontinued because of its irrationality. However, Crivelli uses these deliberately so that everything would contribute to the worshipful image of the Madonna and Child.

14 CARLO CRIVELLI
Madonna and Child Enthroned with Donor
Wood, 129.5 × 54.5 cm
Samuel H. Kress Collection

15 PIETRO PERUGINO
The Crucifixion with the Virgin, Saint John, Saint Jerome and Saint Mary Magdalen
Canvas transferred from wood, Central panel: 101.3 × 56.5 cm, Side panels: 95.2 × 30.5 cm
Andrew W. Mellon Collection

PIETRO PERUGINO
Città della Pieve c 1445 – Fontignano 1523
The Crucifixion with the Virgin, Saint John, Saint Jerome and Saint Mary Magdalen
Plate 15

Although the exquisite landscape background unites the three parts of this painting, it is a reversion to the earlier tryptic type of altarpiece. We are witnessing a devotional meditation on the Crucifixion rather than a representation of the actual event. Christ looks down calmly at the Virgin who, like Saint John, clasps her hands together in an attitude betraying deep emotion, but without any of the profound sorrow she is generally portrayed as showing. Likewise, the saints in the side panels, perhaps to be taken as representing man and womankind, are engaged in mystic communion with Christ. The elegaic mood is perfectly matched in the serene landscape, where everything is painted with

the greatest clarity. The plants in the foreground, many of them there for symbolic reasons, are painted in loving detail. The exact balancing of the figures and the landscape, both forming the arcs of circles, reinforces the mood of calm devotion. The painting once belonged to a Dominican monastery, but it is likely that the donor commissioned the altarpiece for his private chapel, as its small scale would make it unsuitable for any large building. Not surprisingly, the painting was attributed to Raphael. Stylistically it comes close to his early works when he was influenced by Perugino. When the panels were in the Hermitage Museum, in St Petersburg, they were transferred from wood to canvas.

16 LEONARDO DA VINCI
Ginevra de' Benci
Wood 38.2 × 36.7 cm
Ailsa Mellon Bruce Fund

LEONARDO DA VINCI
Vinci 1452 – Cloux, Amboise 1519
Ginevra de' Benci
Plate 16

As the only painting in the United States definitely accredited to Leonardo, there was, of course, much public interest when *Ginevra* was acquired from the Liechtenstein collection in 1967. Leonardo's finished *oeuvre* is remarkably limited for an artist so fertile in ideas, but he suffered from an inability to complete what he had started because the result never satisfied him, and his experimental techniques have further reduced the number of surviving works. Consequently, this portrait, dating from the end of his first Florentine period around 1480, is all the more precious. The painting has been truncated, as the wreath of laurel and palm on the reverse indicates. It is probable that the young lady originally had hands, an adaptation of a pose already created in sculpture by Verrocchio, Leonardo's master. If this is so, and the evidence of Leonardo's drawings at the time strongly suggest it is,

he introduced a new dimension into Italian portraiture. The sitter was the daughter of a rich Florentine banker and supporter of the Medici. At about the period of her portrait, Ginevra had had a love affair with the Venetian ambassador to Florence, Bernardo Bembo, father of the better known humanist Pietro Bembo. The juniper bush behind her is a punning reference to her name. Through the passage of time some colours have changed, the greens turning to brown, and this accounts for the autumnal tone of the background. Ginevra's alabaster-like features have a compelling quality; her eyes are fixed on the beholder and yet seem to pass by him. Her carefully arranged hair is like a torrent coursing over a river bed, and that is not such a surprising comparison as it may seem when we consider Leonardo's interest in water, revealed in his notebooks.

33

Above
17 GIORGIONE
The Adoration of the Shepherds
Wood, 91 × 111 cm
Samuel H. Kress Collection

Right
18 RAPHAEL
Saint George and the Dragon
Wood, 28.5 × 21.5 cm
Andrew W. Mellon Collection

GIORGIONE
Castelfranco c 1478 – Venice 1510
The Adoration of the Shepherds
Plate 17

Giorgione's early death cut short a career of extraordinary promise, yet even in that brief period he had many achievements to his credit. He was already famous in his own lifetime as being the first to paint pictures of secular subjects, appealing to private patrons, rather than religious paintings for public display. Giorgione began the custom of creating art for the pleasure of connoisseurs. We know very little about him and there is a mere handful of paintings attributed to him with certainty. The mystery is deepened by the difficulty of separating the works of Giorgione and the early works of Titian, who in these years was much influenced by him. However, there is a consensus among critics that the *Allendale Adoration*, which is what it has been called after a former owner, is so close to Giorgione's documented works and of such exceptional quality that it can be confidently attributed to him. Around it a further group of paintings, including a *Holy Family* also in the National Gallery, has been

assembled and added to the canon. Giorgione was among the first European painters to introduce landscape as an important mood-creating element in the composition. Indeed, in at least one of his paintings the landscape is more important than the figures. This was a milestone in the emergence of landscape as an independent genre. Here, the beautiful background, gently leading our eye to the distant hills, is certainly based on a region which was familiar to Giorgione, namely his birthplace north of Venice. The landscape enhances the feeling of calm and peace which pervades *The Adoration of the Shepherds*. Through his adoption of oil in addition to tempera as a medium, the colours have an increased luminosity, and this new technique gives greater subtlety to the shadows, eliminating all hard edges. Everything is bathed in a warm, golden light. Giorgione's exquisite sense of colour can be seen in the rich tones of the Virgin's and Saint Joseph's robes – a contrast to those of the shepherds.

RAPHAEL
Urbino 1483 – Rome 1520
Saint George and the Dragon
Plate 18

This little painting has had an adventurous history. It was brought in 1506 by Baldassare Castiglione, the author of that famous manual of courtly life *Il Cortegiano*, as a present to Henry VII of England from Duke Guidobaldo da Montefeltro. Henry had conferred the Order of the Garter on the Duke of Urbino, and Guidobaldo sent an embassy to thank the king. Raphael had been born in Urbino and his father was court painter there. Saint George is the patron of the Order, and the Garter is shown conspicuously on his left leg, while the white horse and rider are compositionally based on the 'George', or jewel, which hangs from the collar worn by the knights. Although small in scale, the painting has been carefully planned so that the prancing horse

counterbalances the diagonal of the lance, and this in turn directs our attention to the dragon. The princess, on whose behalf all this action is taking place, has been relegated to the background, as if she were of minor importance in the scene of combat. Saint George, about whom very little is known, was a third-century martyr, and became the patron of soldiers and of England, so there was a secondary compliment to the king in the subject. When Charles I's collection was sold, after his execution, the *Saint George* passed into the hands of a French connoisseur. It later went to Russia, being bought by Catherine II and there it remained until the early 1930s when the Soviet government disposed of the painting, to obtain foreign currency.

RAPHAEL
The Alba Madonna
Plate 19

Among the many Madonnas painted by Raphael, this is one of the few that is circular. The form was predominantly Florentine and Raphael had just left Florence when he painted the picture. He was never too proud to learn from other artists, and his style, even at the end of his prematurely short career, changed in response to what he admired in his fellow painters. His stay in Florence had opened up to him the great advances Leonardo and Michelangelo had made and his painting became very different from the earlier Peruginesque style. Raphael arrived in Rome in 1508 and shortly afterwards began *The Alba Madonna*. Once more he came under the influence of Michelangelo, then working on the ceiling of the Sistine Chapel. Raphael already knew a Florentine tondo of *The Holy Family* by Michelangelo, and this

must have inspired him to change to a more monumental style. Certainly the Madonna is on an heroic scale, unlike Raphael's earlier paintings of that type, and the Child is deliberately posed to display his muscular body. He might be one of the *ignudi* of the Sistine ceiling. Raphael has also set himself a problem by adopting a round format; this he has solved by making the main contour of the group conform to a lozenge shape, so that none appear to be bursting out of the frame. The Madonna's inclined head and the parallel lines of her right arm and left leg give her a dynamic vigour in contrast to the static quality of Raphael's earlier painting. Before going to the Hermitage Museum, the picture belonged to the Spanish Dukes of Alba, whose name is commemorated in the title.

19 RAPHAEL
The Alba Madonna
Canvas transferred from wood. Diameter 94.5 cm
Andrew W. Mellon Collection

20 GIOVANNI ANTONIO BOLTRAFFIO
Portrait of a Youth
Wood, 46.7 × 35 cm
Ralph and Mary Booth Collection

GIOVANNI ANTONIO BOLTRAFFIO
Milan 1467 – 1516
Portrait of a Youth
Plate 20

A great artist can have an unfortunate as well as a beneficial effect on those coming afterwards. Michelangelo was of such commanding genius that his followers were often overwhelmed by his shadow. The same is true of Leonardo's Milanese assistants, of whom Boltraffio was one. The *sfumato* effect, or subtle change from light to dark, which the older master perfected, often became exaggerated in his pupils, and they tended to copy his models. They found it difficult to emancipate themselves from his powerful influence. In his portrait, Boltraffio demonstrates his debt to Leonardo in the delicate shading of the full cheeks and around the eyes, but at the same time he has succeeded in creating a work of individuality. Other carefully observed details give a special character to the face: the large, thoughtful eyes and the full, almost pouting lips.

ANDREA DEL SARTO
Florence 1486 – 1530
Charity
Plate 21

Michelangelo's enormous influence on his contemporaries is evident in the careful modelling of the nude boys in this group of Charity, which might at first glance be mistaken for a Madonna and Child with Saint John. Andrea del Sarto also adopted Leonardo's use of *sfumato*, which is the gradual transition from light to dark in colours. Here it is controlled, but later the contrasts became more exaggerated and this is an example of Andrea's move away from the classicism of the High Renaissance to Mannerism, a style evolving from the followers of Michelangelo and Raphael. This change comes likewise in the features which

21 ANDREA DEL SARTO
Charity
Wood, 120 × 92.7 cm
Samuel H. Kress Collection

38

no longer conform to the classical ideal. The faces were often viewed from below, as in the child Charity is holding, where the nose has a snout-like form. Del Sarto wished the rhythm of the body to be uniform so he continued the gentle curve of the boy's legs through the body and into the head. The child's glance connects with that of the boy on the left, and he in turn points out of the picture plane as does the boy in the background, thereby including the spectator in the composition. This bouncing backwards and forwards of glance and gesture creates a rhythm as the eye follows the movements, and imparts liveliness to the painting. Andrea del Sarto was unusually sensitive to colour for a Florentine. He employed unexpected combinations such as in Charity's headband and in the tablecloth, while the flamingo dress and yellow sleeves stand out against the dark background.

AGNOLO BRONZINO
Florence 1503 – 1572
A Young Woman and Her Little Boy
Plate 22

One of the characteristics of Mannerism, that style which flourished throughout Europe from the mid-sixteenth century, was an exaggerated height in bodies which was considered to give extra elegance, particularly in portraits. In the same way, as in Bronzino's young lady, the neck was sometimes made exceptionally tall, no doubt to emphasize the subject's aristocratic rank. Her impassive face is an almost perfect oval and the features are exactly balanced. The crescent-shaped arrangement of the hair and the richly-textured cap increase the feeling of remoteness, as if the portrait were no more than an excuse for an exercise in geometry. Even the boy, of whose presence his mother hardly seems aware, has a strangely mask-like face. It would appear that many sitters in this period wished to have only their physical exterior recorded; they did not want to show their inner feelings or give us any clue about what they were thinking. Perhaps the authoritarian atmosphere of Florence, under the restored Medici duke, Cosimo, inhibited free expression. Bronzino has created a splendid image, but we know nothing of the lady's private life.

TITIAN
Pieve di Cadore c 1488 – Venice 1576
Doge Andrea Gritti
Plate 23

Venice in the sixteenth century achieved the summit of its prosperity and greatness. Surviving, as it did, the attacks of a European coalition by land, it succeeded in keeping the powerful Ottoman empire at bay. But the unending war against the Turks was one of the chief causes of Venice's eventual exhaustion, and the signs of decay were already there. Andrea Gritti ruled Venice as doge in these troubled times, and in spite of his great age, he was over 80 when Titian painted him, he took an active role in the fighting. The sense of power and authority is splendidly conveyed in the resolute, almost grim, expression, and in the enormous hand, probably derived from Michelangelo's heroic statue of *Moses*. The great mass of the doge's robe is broken up by the serpentine row of round buttons leading the eye to the forceful head. A brand on the reverse of the painting indicates that it once belonged to Charles I of England.

TITIAN
Venus with a Mirror
Plate 24

In his very long working life Titian painted many nudes. Unlike Michelangelo, who preferred to depict male nudes, Titian and his fellow Venetians gloried in the female body, and never has it been so passionately and sensuously extolled as in their canvases. The debt to Titian continued in nude painting through Rubens and Tiepolo to Renoir, wherever artists have delighted in expressing the creative and procreative forces of nature. Venetian women were often fair-haired and it is these blondes and auburns that Titian used as his models. He has exploited the different textures of Venus' fur and velvet robe, her jewellery and golden braids, and not least her plump milk-white flesh, to give the greatest variety of tactile contrast and visual excitement. X-rays have revealed the changes which Titian made to the *putto* on the extreme right as well as showing that the lower part of the Venus was first clothed in a light chemise. They also tell us that originally Titian had painted portraits of a man and a woman on the canvas, and then, for some reason, had turned it round at right angles and painted over them.

22 AGNOLO BRONZINO
A Young Woman and Her Little Boy
Wood, 99.5 × 76 cm
Widener Collection

40

23 TITIAN
Doge Andrea Gritti
Canvas, 133.6 × 103.2 cm
Samuel H. Kress Collection

24 TITIAN
Venus with a Mirror
Canvas, 124.5 × 105.5 cm
Andrew W. Mellon Collection

JACOPO TINTORETTO
Venice 1518 – 1594
Doge Alvise Mocenigo and Family before the Madonna and Child
Plate 25

No city in Italy has as much official art as Venice. Doges, senators and members of the small group of governing families commissioned quantities of paintings for churches and public buildings, often showing themselves in their robes of office. In Tintoretto's painting, Alvise Mocenigo, doge at the time when victory over the Turks at the battle of Lepanto finally put an end to the threat of invasion, is seen kneeling with his family. Behind him is his brother Giovanni dressed as a senator and behind his wife are two of his nephews. The music-making angels, a traditional feature in Venetian altarpieces, are in fact portraits of his great-nephews. Tintoretto has divided the large painting into three parts to make it more manageable, with the Madonna and Child in the centre and the votive figures in the wings. To offset the unusual width, he has emphasized the verticality through the

Madonna's cloth of honour and the twin columns on either side. The members of the Mocenigo family are distributed regularly in the picture so that their heads, with that of the Madonna, form a W, and there is a secondary rhythm in the arc uniting six of the seven heads. This gives a formality suitable to such a blatant piece of secular propaganda, where a religious subject is made the excuse for a statement of family pride. For some reason, perhaps pressure of business preventing the sitters from visiting Tintoretto's studio, four of the heads were painted on separate pieces of canvas and then stuck on. This may account for a certain disjointedness among the various portraits; the artist must also have relied on studio assistants to complete such a large painting, which may explain some of the unevenness of the painting.

41

PAOLO VERONESE
Verona c 1528 – Venice 1588
The Finding of Moses
Plate 26

Veronese loved to paint rich silks and brocades. His paintings abound in lively, and often extraneous detail. Even his religious subjects are full of light-hearted scenes which he put in because he wanted to; however, a strict reading of the text would not have allowed these. Indeed, he was summoned before the Inquisition and reprimanded for this mixture of the sacred and the profane. It is hard to imagine that this incident from the Old Testament is not set in sixteenth-century Venice and does not depict a great lady walking, surrounded by her attendants, including her dwarf and blackamoor. Yet the event being shown was one of immense importance both to the Jews, who were led by Moses out of captivity in Egypt, and to Christians, for Moses is regarded by them as a forerunner of Christ. Neither of these weighty theological ideas is evident in this scintillating painting. The painting is full of drama, but it is the drama of opera. It is no wonder that Veronese's sparkling and carefree treatment of whatever he painted appealed to eighteenth-century taste, and in Venice it helped to produce the last creative burst of that school under Tiepolo.

43

27 GIOVANNI BATTISTA MORONI
A Gentleman in Adoration before the Madonna
Canvas, 60 × 65 cm
Samuel H. Kress Collection

GIOVANNI BATTISTA MORONI
Bergamo c 1520 – 1578
A Gentleman in Adoration before the Madonna
Plate 27

Even though Venetian art predominated within the Venetian republic, the provincial centres, often with long traditions of autonomy, continued to exist culturally on their own. Moroni worked in Bergamo and its surrounding district. He produced religious works, but his relaxed and objective portraits are of greater interest. In this combined portrait and devotional painting there is a strange discrepancy between the scale of the praying man and the Madonna and Child, and the two sections are painted in a different style. Perhaps the religious figures are intended to be a

vision, or possibly a statue. The gentle pathos of the Madonna and Child, so close to Lorenzo Lotto, who also worked in Bergamo, are in contrast with the realism of the suppliant whose embroidered collar and cuff stand out strikingly from his black velvet jacket and scarlet sleeve.

28 DOSSO DOSSI
Circe and Her Lovers in a Landscape
Canvas, 100.8 × 136.1 cm
Samuel H. Kress Collection

DOSSO DOSSI
Ferrara active 1512 – 1542
Circe and Her Lovers in a Landscape
Plate 28

Outside the main creative centres of Florence, Rome and Venice, many other towns produced important and distinctive art. Ferrara, under its cultivated d' Este dukes, provided extensive patronage, and a flourishing school of painting had existed there since the fourteenth century. The dukes also commissioned works from outside their dominions: Bellini's *The Feast of the Gods* is an example. Dosso Dossi also helped to decorate Alfonso d' Este's study and painted many works for him. Circe, as related in Homer's *Odyssey*, was an enchantress who changed Odysseus' companions into swine when they landed on her island. Dossi used instead the version in *Orlando Furioso* by Ariosto, the court poet of Ferrara. There is nothing horrific in this story in which the sailors were transformed into various animals and birds, remaining apparently quite content with their changed state and forced captivity. They have gathered round the enchantress who is declaiming from a tablet; a book of magic lies at her feet. Titian's influence is apparent in the nude Circe, seen as a beautiful nymph. The idyllic sunset landscape and general air of calm pervading the picture owe much to Giorgione. The strange twilight and curious stillness of the creatures, who seem to have been immobilized by a spell, help to create a magical atmosphere, making Circe's power quite credible.

45

29 BACCHIACCA
The Gathering of Manna
Wood, 112 × 95 cm
Samuel H. Kress Collection

BACCHIACCA
Florence 1495 – 1557
The Gathering of Manna
Plate 29

Florentine Mannerism benefited from the patronage of the restored Medici dynasty which wished to further the prestige of its new title, that of duke, by encouraging the arts. The influence of his great compatriots Michelangelo and Andrea del Sarto is evident in Bacchiacca's paintings. This is one of a pair; the other, showing Moses striking a rock to obtain water, is in Edinburgh. Both illustrate episodes in the journey of the Children of Israel in the wilderness. The exotic setting has provided Bacchiacca with an excuse to paint wild beasts such as the giraffe, the bear, a pair of lynxes and a porcupine. In a similar way, the fantastic head-dresses are a traditional means of indicating the foreign origin of the Jews, who still had to wear a special costume in those European countries where they were allowed to live. A further example of the Mannerist love of the unusual can be seen in the vessels the people were commanded to bring for the gathering of manna. Each one has a different shape and they might all serve as patterns for the metal-worker's art. The painter has flattened the space through the curious ridges in the middle distance, cutting off some of the figures, and the hills climb up the composition in a way reminiscent of Northern European landscape painting. The grey complexions and acid colours are characteristic of Bacchiacca's style, as are the elegant and elaborately posed figures.

JAN VAN EYCK
Maseyck? c 1380 – Bruges 1441
The Annunciation
Plate 30

This painting, which originally hung in the Hermitage, is a wing of a lost altarpiece which was transferred, in the nineteenth century, from wood to canvas; in the process some of the paint from the Madonna's robe may have been damaged, but otherwise the condition is excellent. Only a close examination of the original can reveal the miraculous details of the angel's sceptre, jewelled and brocaded robe, and crown. Van Eyck was particularly interested in light and could paint its fall on objects with the most amazing accuracy and subtlety. Light also created a rational space in which van Eyck's figures could move convincingly. The use of oil gave an added brilliance to his colours, so that contemporaries were impressed by the life-like quality of his paintings. In *The Annunciation*, van Eyck deliberately broke the natural laws of light by showing two sources in the same composition. The source of natural light is from the right, while the supernatural light comes from the opposite direction, on the Virgin's right, which was the side of honour. There are many elements of symbolism in the painting; to give a few instances: throughout the church, on the floor tiles and the walls, there are scenes from the Old Testament associated with the coming of Christ, and the three windows behind the Virgin represent the Trinity. The medieval world constantly looked for allegories and symbols in the most everyday occurrences, so it is not surprising to find them in a painting depicting an event of such significance. The brightly-coloured figures stand out against the subdued church interior, the Virgin's traditional blue robe relieved only by a narrow scarlet belt. She has been interrupted at prayer and is shown anachronistically in a Christian church.

ROGER VAN DER WEYDEN
Tournai? c 1400 – Brussels 1464
Portrait of a Lady
Plate 31

Roger van der Weyden's robust and realistic style contrasts with the refined courtly manner of van Eyck, the other founder of the Flemish school, and his influence continued long after his death. The main development of fifteenth-century Flemish portraiture was the introduction of half-lengths showing the hands, an innovation that Italian painters were later to adopt. This, together with the use of oil paint, gives a greater immediacy and naturalism to the portraits. Roger's very human approach is well brought out in this sympathetic treatment of a rather plain young woman. The face is softly modelled, light playing evenly over the features and defining the contours. Her face is framed by a wimple and is painted with the highest technical skill. Only a red belt brings a stronger note into the subdued colour of her dress, while the gold buckle and rings introduce an air of luxury. It is a restful and comforting portrait; the young girl is lost in thought, her clasped hands forming an intricate pattern as she appears to rest them on the edge of the frame. Van der Weyden . painted a similar portrait, now in the National Gallery, London.

ROGER VAN DER WEYDEN
Saint George and the Dragon
Plate 32

This astonishing painting, no larger than an illuminated page in a Book of Hours and almost requiring a magnifying glass to appreciate all its beauties, has also been attributed by connoisseurs to one or other of the brothers Hubert or Jan van Eyck. The general feeling now is that Roger painted it, but the van Eyck influence is certainly strong in the elegance of the figures and the horse. Saint George is treated like a knight from the Burgundian court equipped for jousting at one of those elaborate tournaments so popular in the late Middle Ages, the princess acting the part of his lady. The saint's lance, creating a dramatic diagonal, is about to deliver the death blow to the dragon. The detailed treatment of the landscape is almost incredible on such a minute scale. Two riders approach a town overlooked by a fantastic rock and castle. The towers of the town wall are reflected in the water, while further out, two ships sail in from the sea. Roger has conjured up a magical world which is perfectly believable.

33 MASTER OF HEILIGENKREUZ
The Death of Saint Clare
Wood, 66.4 × 54.5 cm
Samuel H. Kress Collection

MASTER OF HEILIGENKREUZ
First half fifteenth century
The Death of Saint Clare
Plate 33

At one stage it was thought that the anonymous painter of this panel might be French, but now he is more generally believed to be Austrian or Bohemian. In the period when he was working, an international style predominated in Europe, and this often makes it difficult to be certain of a painting's origin, especially when many artists were itinerant and worked in several countries. The elegance and refinement of French medieval art, which influenced painting and sculpture throughout Europe, is observable in the richly dressed saints, with their attenuated fingers, grouped round Saint Clare's death-bed. They might be court ladies in their fashionable clothes. The brilliant colours,

decorative haloes and tooled gold background all enhance this feeling of splendour, rather at odds with the poverty vowed by Saint Clare and her nuns in the thirteenth-century. Clare was a close follower of Saint Francis of Assisi, and founded the second order of Franciscans called the Poor Clares; her nuns led a life of great austerity. According to legend, on her death-bed Clare was visited by the Virgin and various saints, while Christ appeared to receive her soul.

MASTER OF THE SAINT LUCY LEGEND
Flemish active 1480 – 89
Mary, Queen of Heaven
Plate 34

This altarpiece comes from a Spanish convent and was probably painted by a Flemish artist from Bruges. Many Flemish altarpieces were imported into Spain and influenced painting there. The subject, Mary's ascent to Heaven, is a joyous one and the angels welcome her with vocal and instrumental music. There is also the atmosphere of a court, for the Virgin will be crowned as queen by the enthroned Trinity waiting for her at the top of the

painting. The vibrant colours and rich materials of the clothes worn by the celestial beings contrast with the subdued earthly landscape below. Mary's ascent has been treated as a mixture of an Assumption, a Coronation and an Immaculate Conception, each quite separate themes. The last was of particular interest in Spain, where the Virgin had a strong cult, and the belief was widely held there long before it became official dogma.

HIERONYMUS BOSCH
's Hertogenbosch c 1450 – 1516
Death and the Miser
Plate 35

The seven deadly sins frequently formed the subject of medieval paintings, and the dreadful effects of avarice, in this world and the next, were constant themes of sermons and books of devotion. No matter how wicked a man had been, it was still possible for him to be saved if he repented at the moment of death. Although the decision must be made consciously by the dying sinner, moralists thought of this momentous choice as a literal struggle between the forces of good and evil for a man's soul. In Bosch's painting, which must have formed the wing of a larger work, the miser is shown on his sick-bed, with Death about to throw his dart. An angel exhorts the man to confide himself to Christ. He looks up

at the crucifix in the window, but his hand moves towards the money-bag offered by the demon. This ambivalence is also found in the foreground scene where the miser, this time still able to conduct business, fingers a rosary, yet he is carefully adding to his treasure. The meaning of the painting is fairly obvious, but in many of Bosch's paintings the allusions to contemporary proverbs and allegories are so dense that present day viewers often find difficulty in understanding them. One thing we can be sure of, however amusing or quaint some of the details in Bosch's works may seem, his intentions were of the utmost seriousness. The choice between heaven and hell was not a laughing matter.

34 MASTER OF THE SAINT LUCY LEGEND
Mary, Queen of Heaven
Wood, 215.9 × 185.4 cm
Samuel H. Kress Collection

GERARD DAVID
Oudewater c 1460 – Bruges 1523
The Rest on the Flight into Egypt
Plate 36

The traditional Flemish style continued into the sixteenth century in Bruges at a time when the influence of the Italian Renaissance made itself felt in Antwerp and established it as the leading centre of painting, just as in commerce the older city ceded place to its younger rival. Following on from his master, Memling, David filled his paintings with details which relate the religious scenes to everyday life. The landscape here is supposed to be Egyptian, but it is obviously Flemish. In the foreground are several plants, each easily identifiable. Some have a special symbolism: the violet and fern represent humility; the cyclamen, the sorrows of the Virgin; and the strawberry signifying righteousness. As is often the case with scenes from the childhood of Christ, there are prefigurations of his Passion, not only in the flowers, but also in the bunch of grapes he is holding. There is a long gap in the New Testament between Christ's birth and the beginning of his ministry. This blank was filled with apocryphal stories. The flight into Egypt to escape Herod's wrath is recorded, but various legends grew up about the journey there. According to one, when Mary was hungry, Joseph could not gather dates until Jesus commanded the palm to lower its branches. David has altered this to fit in with the European setting and Joseph hits the branches of a chestnut tree. It could be any ordinary family resting on a journey with their beautifully painted wicker basket in the foreground. Yet there is at the same time a sweetness in the figures, so well matched in the peaceful landscape, which creates a feeling of harmony.

MATHIS GRÜNEWALD
Würzburg c 1465 – Halle 1528
The Small Crucifixion
Plate 37

Grünewald was obviously a deeply religious man and he survived into the early years of the Reformation, becoming a supporter of Luther. Yet he continued to draw on the medieval tradition of German art and piety, simple, emotional and frequently tending to mysticism. Anyone who has seen Grünewald's greatest work, the Isenheim altarpiece, must have come away with an unforgettable aesthetic and religious experience and must be convinced that he is one of the masters of sixteenth-century European painting. The representation of the Crucifixion in German art spared none of the horrific details which Italian painters tended to glide over. In no sense could Christ's tortured body in this painting be regarded as a glorification of the classical ideal, such as would have appeared in contemporary Italian art. The body is broken and misshapen with the weals and thorns from the scourging plainly visible: the intense suffering is overwhelming. The hands of the Virgin and Saint John are clasped tight in their grief, like knots which will never come untied; the jagged edges of their clothes underline the poignancy and agony of despair. A black sky, with a moon in eclipse, adds to this hopeless feeling as if illustrating the mystical 'dark night of the soul' sometimes felt by the most devout.

Left
35 HIERONYMUS BOSCH
Death and the Miser
Wood, 93 × 31 cm
Samuel H. Kress Collection

Right
36 GERARD DAVID
The Rest on the Flight into Egypt
Wood, 45 × 44.5 cm
Andrew W. Mellon Collection

Below Right
37 MATHIS GRÜNEWALD
The Small Crucifixion
Wood, 61.6 × 46 cm
Samuel H. Kress Collection

LUCAS CRANACH THE ELDER
Kronach 1472 – Weimar 1553
A Prince of Saxony
Plate 38

For many years Cranach lived at the court of the Elector of Saxony and painted portraits of his patron Frederick the Wise, the protector of Luther, and his family. Cranach was also a supporter of the Reformation and provided some of its pictorial propaganda. Yet, unlike Grünewald, it does not seem to have disturbed him unduly. His view of the world was more pedestrian and materialistic. He excelled in portraying what he saw, as can be seen here in the texture of the prince's hair and the rich stuffs which make up his costume. But, in spite of the elaborate clothing, it is still very much the portrait of a boy, and Cranach has caught the wistful expression of childhood which is found at all social levels. The figure stands out in sharp contrast to the dark background. The prince wears, somewhat casually, a crown of rue referring to the chief emblem on the Saxon coat of arms. We are not sure which member of the electoral family he was. His sister's portrait by Cranach is also in the National Gallery of Art.

ALBRECHT DÜRER
Nuremberg 1471 – 1528
Portrait of a Clergyman
Plate 39

Dürer took both himself and his art very seriously. He was supremely conscious of the status of painters, who in Germany still ranked among the artisans, and aspired to raise them to the level enjoyed by their Italian contemporaries. He visited Venice twice and met Giovanni Bellini, who made a deep impression on him. Dürer became the medium through which Renaissance art reached Germany. Like Leonardo, who certainly influenced him, he wished to be considered as an all-round humanist rather than a mere painter. He moved in literary circles and wrote treatises on painting, fortifications, mathematics and other subjects. Painting was only one side of Dürer's artistic output; his very large production of woodcuts and engravings are perhaps his greatest achievement and he ranks among the foremost graphic artists. Dürer's imaginative range combined the late Gothic tradition of the North with the classical ideas of the Italian Renaissance. The Gothic influence is still strong in this portrait of a clergyman. Instead of the features being generalized, every detail is painted with equal clarity, so that each strand of hair seems to have a separate existence. The eyes stare with almost painful intensity, and this may be a reflection more of the artist's neurotic temperament than the sitter's personality. The face has a craggy look, the hard contours of the cheeks and jaw barely modelled by light and standing in clear relief. Dürer's acute observation is apparent in the reflection of a window, possibly one in the artist's studio, in the pupils of the eyes. The clergyman is almost certainly Johann Dorsch, an Augustinian canon who became a Lutheran; he lived in Nuremberg and preached at Dürer's funeral, which took place at his church. Dürer was friendly with several Reformers, including Luther, and the subject has sometimes been identified as the Swiss Reformer, Zwingli, whom Dürer also knew.

HANS HOLBEIN THE YOUNGER
Augsburg 1497 – London 1543
Edward VI as a Child
Plate 40

The court of Henry VIII, and the king himself and his various wives, are immortalized by Holbein, who had originally come to England with an introduction from Erasmus to Sir Thomas More. Perhaps his position as a foreigner, and a Lutheran sympathizer, made Holbein wary of declaring himself too openly in the tortuous political atmosphere of England at a time of change, and his sitters seem equally determined not to reveal more than was necessary of their inner thoughts. His paintings are superbly finished, but compared with his drawings, done from life, they lack a certain spontaneity. Regal portraits are images and statements of power, so that this loss would not be so important in them. Even royal infants were treated with the deference given to their elders, and although only 14 months old, the Prince of Wales is richly dressed in a cloth of gold and scarlet and holds a gold rattle; he has the red hair of his father and an indication of the same determination in the chin. Henry VIII had broken with the Pope and caused a social revolution, through the dissolution of the monasteries, in his desire to have a son to succeed him on the throne. The birth of the prince was therefore of the greatest importance to the future of England and many hopes and fears were centred around his young head. The king must have been happy to receive the portrait as a New Year's gift from the artist in 1539. The Latin verses exhort the prince to follow the path of virtue and to be a good ruler. Alas for all Henry's dynastic plans, Edward did succeed his father, but he died at the age of 15.

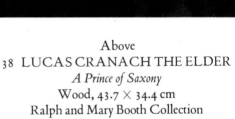

Above
38 LUCAS CRANACH THE ELDER
A Prince of Saxony
Wood, 43.7 × 34.4 cm
Ralph and Mary Booth Collection

Above Right
39 ALBRECHT DÜRER
Portrait of a Clergyman
Vellum mounted on canvas 42.9 × 33.2 cm
Samuel H. Kress Collection

Right
40 HANS HOLBEIN THE YOUNGER
Edward VI as a Child
Wood, 57 × 44 cm
Andrew W. Mellon Collection

41 JAN GOSSAERT, CALLED MABUSE
Portrait of a Banker
Wood, 63.6 × 47.5 cm
Ailsa Mellon Bruce Fund

JAN GOSSAERT, CALLED MABUSE
Mauberge c 1478 – Antwerp c 1533
Portrait of a Banker
Plate 41

The beginnings of modern banking had been established in the Middle Ages by Italians, but at the time this portrait was painted the commercial centre of Europe had moved to the southern part of the Netherlands, to what is now Belgium. This area was in a more advantageous position than the Mediterranean for the new trade routes which opened up the Atlantic, the New World and the East. The medieval restrictions on usury and interest, always easy to circumvent, had largely disappeared even before the Reformation, which is often associated with the rise of modern capitalism. There is, consequently, no element of satire in the portrait. Mabuse shows a merchant banker surrounded by his papers, ledger and other equipment of his honourable profession,

all painted with precision. This attention to detail is part of the artist's Netherlandish heritage. But he also came under Italian influence through a visit to Rome, and the massiveness of the figure, brought so far forward in the picture plane, suggests a knowledge of contemporary southern portraiture. The banker's puffed up sleeves introduce a dashing note of fashion into the costume, and the painter has carefully followed all the intricacies of their folds. The hands are sensitive and those of a gentleman. In fact, initials on one of the rings and on the hat badge almost certainly identify the man as Jeronimus Sandelin, a tax collector in Zeeland, who later had a distinguished career in the fiscal administration.

42 FRANÇOIS CLOUET
'Diane de Poitiers'
Wood, 92.1 × 81.3 cm
Samuel H. Kress Collection

FRANÇOIS CLOUET
Tours c 1510 – Paris 1572
'Diane de Poitiers'
Plate 42

The lady taking a bath was once thought to be Diane de Poitiers, mistress of Henry II of France, but this is no longer held to be so. It has also been suggested that the painting is a Huguenot satire on Mary Queen of Scots. There certainly appear to be many allegorical details in the painting, whose meaning is not clear. The lady does bear a resemblance to the young queen who was painted by Clouet in her widowhood before returning to Scotland. The child being suckled by the wet nurse could be the queen's young son James VI of Scotland, later James I of England, whose father was murdered under mysterious circumstances, probably with Mary's connivance. The unicorn embroidered on the chair back may be a reference to the supporters of the arms of Scotland, and a satirical commentary on Mary's morals, for the mythical beast was associated with virginity. Clouet came from a family of Netherlandish painters and he succeeded his father as portraitist to the king of France. He was also influenced by the Italian artists imported to work at the French court, and it is possible he himself travelled to Italy. These two traditions are combined here with the Leonardesque female nude representing the southern style and the peasant woman and the carefully painted still-life details stemming from the northern tradition. Both are combined to form a highly-sophisticated work. The painting is signed, which is rare in Clouet's work.

EL GRECO (DOMENIKOS THEOTOKOPOULOS)
Crete 1541 – Toledo 1614
Saint Martin and the Beggar
Plate 43

El Greco, which is the nickname given to Domenikos Theotokopoulos in Spain, was born in Crete, at that time part of the Venetian empire. He studied in Venice, possibly with Titian, before going to Spain where he spent most of his working life; thus, there were at least three distinct elements in his artistic formation. In a curious way his very personal style, a mixture of residual Byzantine formalism and Italian Mannerism, matched the religious climate, often ecstatic and mystical, of Counter-Reformation Spain. Saint Martin's famous act of charity, when as a Roman soldier he divided his cloak with a beggar, was a popular subject in art, for he was venerated throughout Europe. The saint lived in fourth century France, but El Greco has made him into an elegant young Spanish nobleman of around 1600. The painting, as is the case with many of El Greco's works, has unusually narrow proportions. This emphasized the elongation of the figures, which also have the exaggeratedly long faces, necks and hands typical of El Greco. Also typical are the acid colours, especially the brilliant blue. El Greco has signed his name in Greek. A smaller version of Saint Martin and the Beggar is also in the National Gallery's collection.

EL GRECO
Laocoön
Plate 44

When the Laocoön was discovered in Rome in 1506 it was recognized as a long-lost Greek sculpture known from Pliny's description, and it quickly became a famous model for artists to use in their compositions when they wished to express strong emotion under suffering. El Greco has not, however, adapted the Laocoön for its classical poses, but concentrated on the pathos of the tragedy. The priest Laocoön had warned the Trojans against the danger of the wooden horse, seen here in the background, thereby offending the god Apollo who sent serpents to kill him and his two sons. El Greco has deliberately rejected the accepted canons of classical proportion and substituted his own. The two central figures sprawl in ungainly fashion, while the third victim, exaggeratedly slender, seems to be engaged in a gymnastic exercise. The legs are unusually long and the bodies with their bulging muscles lack the smooth lines demanded by classical decorum. El Greco has also used an unnatural flesh tone, giving an almost corpse-like pallor. On the right are a young man and woman (a pentimento is clearly visible in her head which once turned the other way) with attenuated limbs, who are spectators of the god's terrible vengeance. The city in the distance, under the tenebrous, flickering sky, is not Troy but recognizably Toledo where El Greco worked for much of his life. The painting once belonged to Prince Paul, Regent of Yugoslavia at the time of the Second World War.

60

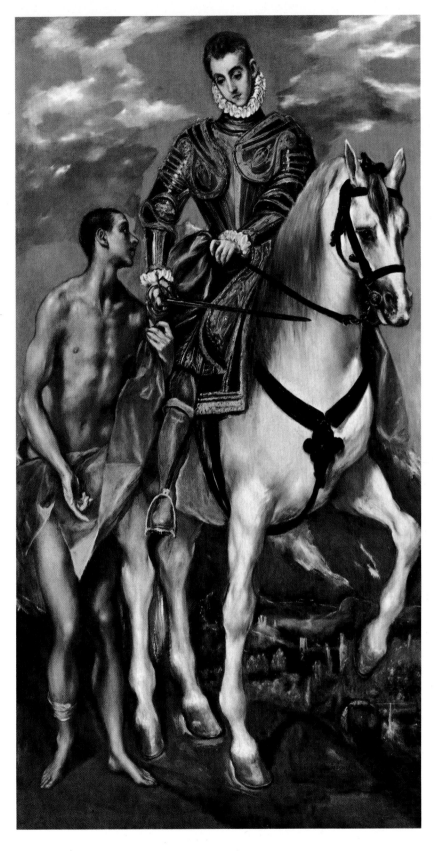

43 EL GRECO (DOMENIKOS THEOTOKOPOULOS)
Saint Martin and the Beggar
Canvas, 193.5 × 103 cm
Widener Collection

Above
44 EL GRECO
Laocoön
Canvas, 137.5 × 172.5 cm
Samuel H. Kress Collection

Left
45 DIEGO VELÁZQUEZ
The Needlewoman
Canvas, 74 × 60 cm
Andrew W. Mellon Collection

DIEGO VELÁZQUEZ
Seville 1599 – Madrid 1660
The Needlewoman
Plate 45

Velázquez was the first painter, produced by the Spanish school, of any European importance – El Greco was a Cretan by birth. He made two visits to Italy, but Italian paintings, especially those by Titian, were well represented in the royal collection. Velázquez, as court painter, knew them intimately, so that all he needed to form his style was at hand. Kings, princesses, courtiers and dwarfs, the whole range of Spanish society in its golden age,

passes before us in the canvases of Velázquez. We do not know who the sitter is in this unfinished portrait; she is sometimes said to be the painter's daughter Francesca. He has painted in the forms of the face and body with masterly economy, every brush stroke performing its task and none redundant. It is this vigorous style which makes Velázquez's work so exciting and which made it appeal to Manet and his contemporaries.

FRANCISCO ZURBARÁN
Fuente de Cantos 1598 – Madrid 1664
Saint Jerome with Saint Paula and Saint Eustochium
Plate 46

Few painters have equalled the austere grandeur in Zurbarán's religious works. The simple devotion of contemporary Spain is reflected in his many paintings of saints, often repeated several times, who are depicted with such realism that we might take them for portraits. Here, Saint Jerome, one of the Doctors of the Church and the translator of the Bible into Latin, is sitting with his followers, Saint Paula, a rich and noble Roman lady, and her daughter Saint Eustochium. The scene is intended to be

Jerusalem, where all three spent much of their lives. Zurbarán has divided the composition into two parts, the women seated in front of an opening, while Jerome is against a dark background. His dramatic gesture unites the two halves. The painting is also unified through the brown and white habits of the figures, the only brighter colour being the red leather of Saint Paula's chair and Saint Jerome's scarlet cape and cardinal's hat, one of his identifying attributes.

BARTOLOMÉ ESTEBAN MURILLO
Seville 1617 – 1682
The Return of the Prodigal Son
Plate 47

It is hard to resist the appeal of this joyful painting with its bright and cheerful colours which match the happy scene as a reunited father and son greet each other affectionately. On another level this can be interpreted as the Church welcoming back a penitent heretic. Murillo obviously enjoyed painting the various textures of the materials, even the prodigal son's rags have been rendered with great dash. The whole composition is transferred into a genre scene of people about to celebrate a feast. Like most

Spanish painters of his day, Murillo produced mainly religious pictures, and his sweet and undemanding style achieved considerable popularity. His series of Madonnas have been reproduced so often that they now rate among the best known religious paintings of any period. He was one of the first Spanish artists to be known outside his own country and had some influence on eighteenth-century English painting, notably on Hogarth and Gainsborough.

ORAZIO GENTILESCHI
Pisa 1563 – London 1639
The Lute Player
Plate 48

Caravaggio's influence was felt strongly by contemporary and later day artists, not only in his use of dramatic lighting, but also in his choice of subject matter. He painted several pictures with musical subjects. Gentileschi moved to Rome shortly after Caravaggio's departure and he absorbed many elements of the latter's style. When the Prince of Liechtenstein acquired the painting, the artist was correctly identified, even though the closeness to Caravaggio later suggested an attribution to him, a mistake which long persisted. The strongly-lighted white blouse

and gold dress stand out against the dark background. The same light which falls on the girl illuminates the lower corner of the table-cloth, but leaves the rest in shadow. There is also a shaft of light in the upper left-hand corner of the painting and this diagonal starts a series of zigzag rhythms which echo through the composition, in the arms, neck, thighs and legs of the player as well as in the sections of the lute. There is an array of musical instruments on the table and some sheet music that make up a pleasing still-life.

Left
46 FRANCISCO ZURBARÁN
Saint Jerome with Saint Paula and Saint Eustochium
Canvas, 245.1 × 173 cm
Samuel H. Kress Collection

Below
47 BARTOLOMÉ ESTEBAN MURILLO
The Return of the Prodigal Son
Canvas, 236.3 × 261 cm
Gift of the Avalon Foundation

Left
48 ORAZIO GENTILESCHI
The Lute Player
Canvas, 143.5 × 128.8 cm
Ailsa Mellon Bruce Fund

Below
49 PETER PAUL RUBENS
Daniel in the Lions' Den
Canvas, 224.3 × 330.4 cm
Ailsa Mellon Bruce Fund

PETER PAUL RUBENS
Siegen 1577 – Antwerp 1640
Daniel in the Lions' Den
Plate 49

Rubens achieved European fame, not only through his paintings for which demands came from many countries, but also as a diplomat. He went on several embassies on behalf of the Duke of Mantua and the rulers of the Spanish Netherlands and lived in considerable style. In order to satisfy all the requests for his paintings and also because he could not devote all his time to his art, he had inevitably to rely on the assistance of his studio, especially for larger works. Rubens would make a sketch and perhaps a small-scale *modello*, which his rapid manner of working enabled him to do with ease, and then his well-trained pupils were able to convert these into the finished picture. Many artists, who later made an independent name for themselves, worked as pupils of Rubens, so even studio production was of considerable quality. The master himself frequently made corrections and alterations. It is especially valuable, however, to know that

Rubens painted the *Daniel* entirely by himself. Sir Dudley Carleton, English ambassador at The Hague, bought the painting for Charles I and the artist confirmed that the picture was entirely from his own hand. For many years the painting hung in the boardroom of an English business firm, disregarded as a copy. It did not become apparent that it was a lost original until after the picture had been sold.

Rubens was one of the finest nude painters, and has given Daniel an athletic body rippling with muscles. The pink flesh is illuminated by the hole above and stands out against the murky recesses of the den. The lions are carefully posed from different angles and are based on studies Rubens had made from lions in the local menagerie. One of these drawings is also in the National Gallery. One lion seems to be parodying Daniel's uplifted face and plaintive expression as he waits for the Lord to rescue him.

RUBENS
Deborah Kip, Wife of Sir Balthasar Gerbier, and Her Children
Plate 50

Balthasar Gerbier played an important part in the artistic and political world of England under Charles I. Born in Holland of Huguenot parents, and trained as a miniature painter, Gerbier was a noted connoisseur and helped to acquire paintings for his patron the Duke of Buckingham, Charles I's favourite. After the duke's assassination, he passed into the king's service. Gerbier also used his collecting activities as a cover for diplomatic intrigues and eventually became English agent in Brussels. It was in this way that he met Rubens, who also combined painting and diplomacy, although on a far higher level than Gerbier. The two became friends, and when Rubens visited London in 1629 on a peace mission, he stayed with Gerbier. At that time, Rubens

painted his host's wife, the daughter of a Dutch merchant in London, and her family. He must have been reminded of his own first wife and their three children. Originally, the painting consisted of just the heads of the mother and her children, but later Rubens added strips on all four sides to include the grander setting of the columns, mermaid caryatids forming an arbour, and the landscape background. These give increased monumentality, but the painting remains very much a study of motherhood, like the traditional image of Charity nursing a group of infants. Rubens was so impressed with the little girl in the centre that he repeated the figure in his painting *War and Peace* which hangs in the National Gallery, London.

ANTON VAN DYCK
Antwerp 1599 – London 1641
Marchesa Grimaldi, Wife of Marchese Nicola Cattaneo
Plate 51

Genoa was a mercantile republic but its ruling families were every bit as exclusive and conscious of their birth as the nobility in the other European countries. In the portraits painted during his youthful stay in Genoa, van Dyck captured this aristocratic hauteur which strongly influenced his style. The figures were often made exaggeratedly tall to give them a more imposing character, while the grand settings and rich, sombre colours created a suitably dignified atmosphere. Genoa also introduced van Dyck to more complex, not to say devious personalities than he had hitherto encountered, and his psychological penetration

became more subtle as a result. The marchesa, a member of one of the leading Genoese families, stands majestically upright as her little black page holds a red sun-shade over her; this provides the only major patch of colour in the painting, acting as a backdrop to her pale face. Originally, as indicated in a drawing, van Dyck had planned to include the marchesa's little daughter in the portrait, but she was excluded from the painting. Instead, she was painted separately and her portrait, together with one of her brother, is also in the National Gallery, which has an outstanding collection of van Dycks from his Genoese period.

50 RUBENS
Deborah Kip, Wife of Sir Balthasar Gerbier, and Her Children
Canvas, 165.8 × 177.8 cm
Andrew W. Mellon Fund

VAN DYCK
Philip, Lord Wharton
Plate 52

Charles I had a great love of painting and wished to attract foreign artists to England. Van Dyck became his court painter and spent the last nine years of his life there. The king was fortunate to secure him, for the brilliant and ephemeral Caroline court, soon to be broken up by the Civil War, is recorded forever in van Dyck's portraits. Nothing like them had been seen in England before, the native tradition being a watered-down version of Flemish painting engrafted on residual Holbein, which was hopelessly provincial and van Dyck had no difficulty in making it seem quite out of date. It is not surprising that his canvases, with their elegant assurance, established a traditional style that survived in English painting, especially for official and grand-manner portraiture, down to the present century, and is not even dead today. The conceit of ladies and gentlemen dressing up as simple country-folk was common both in literature and painting from the Renaissance. No one would be deceived into

thinking this young nobleman could be a shepherd; he was rather, an ornament of Charles I's court, although he later went into opposition to the king. At an advanced age he became a duke. The shepherd's scoop he carries so gracefully symbolizes the virtues of pastoral life. The delights of rustic existence have a long tradition in Europe and continued down to the time of Marie-Antoinette and her milkmaids at Versailles. Such illusions were rudely shattered by the French Revolution, just as Charles I's dreams perished in the Civil War. Van Dyck produced the images that English aristocrats wanted to see of themselves, and he became immensely popular. The portraits are seldom penetrating, but they reflect the self confidence and animal spirits of the ruling class. Lord Wharton has the charm and good looks of youth, able to anticipate a life of ease and privilege. His portrait once belonged to Sir Robert Walpole, the British Prime Minister, and later joined the collection of Catherine II of Russia.

51 ANTON VAN DYCK
Marchesa Grimaldi, Wife of Marchese Nicola Cattaneo
Canvas, 246.4 × 172.7 cm
Widener Collection

52 VAN DYCK
Philip, Lord Wharton
Canvas, 133 × 106 cm
Widener Collection

FRANS HALS
Antwerp c 1580 – Haarlem 1666
Portrait of an Elderly Lady
Plate 53

It is unfortunate for Hals that he is often compared, to his disadvantage, with his great contemporary Rembrandt. But the aims of the two painters were not the same. Where Rembrandt's tones were generally subdued and his colours in the darker range, Hals' were frequently lively and bathed in strong light. He was also less interested in psychological depth and concentrated on externals, catching the fleeting expression on his sitter's face like a cloud passing over the sun. His brushwork is spirited and fluid, and it is not surprising that some of the first generation of French Impressionists became excited about Hals' technical virtuosity. He could convey the utmost brilliance even when his colours were confined to black, grey and white. The whole surface becomes a dazzling display of brushwork. Hals' best-known portraits are those of swashbuckling officers from the companies

raised to fight for Dutch independence against Spain. This does him a disservice because it distorts the impression of his style. He could also paint more restrained portraits, especially in his later years when he had fallen on bad times and depended on charity. The sympathetic depiction of this elderly lady's face – 60 was a considerable age in the seventeenth century – does not conceal the marks of time in her lines and wrinkles. Her gnarled hands are highlighted against the black dress and, although her fingers are twisted, she still grasps the arm of the chair vigorously. She is probably holding a Bible or some book of devotion, for the Dutch were pious, and there is a calm confidence in the lady's face suggesting the inner peace given by religion. The National Gallery has eight portraits by Hals, but this is the only one of a woman.

53 FRANS HALS
Portrait of an Elderly Lady
Canvas, 103 × 86.4 cm
Andrew W. Mellon Collection

54 REMBRANDT VAN RIJN
Self-Portrait
Canvas, 84 × 66 cm
Andrew W. Mellon Collection

REMBRANDT VAN RIJN
Leyden 1606 – Amsterdam 1669
Self-Portrait
Plate 54

There are few artists who painted themselves as frequently as Rembrandt; self-portraits make up nearly a tenth of his total production, spanning his entire career. Few have been so honest in their record of poverty, age and neglect. The later self-portraits are almost unbearably revealing, but there is never any demand for our pity. An unquenchable faith in himself, and a refusal to be defeated by the fickleness of his public or the vagaries of life, appear in all the faces that look out unflinchingly from his canvases. Rembrandt's earlier life had been prosperous and successful, and his wife Saskia had brought him a considerable dowry. After she died, things began to go wrong for Rembrandt. His extravagant life, and changing public taste leading to fewer commissions, made him a bankrupt in 1656. This self-portrait is dated three years after this, but Rembrandt still presents himself without shame or any attempt at evasion; his eyes may be care-worn, but they refuse to despair. He has modelled the face with economy, using broad brush strokes, and the hands are barely indicated. For the curls of his hair he used the point of the brush. Such variations in texture in the same painting are typical; he would even use his fingers to give greater expression to the paint. The dark background and sombre clothing offset the more strongly-lit face, almost glowing with an inner light. A slightly earlier self-portrait is also in the Gallery.

Top Left
55 REMBRANDT VAN RIJN
The Apostle Paul
Canvas, 129 × 102 cm
Widener Collection

Top Right
56 REMBRANDT VAN RIJN
Portrait of a Lady with an Ostrich-Feather Fan
Canvas, 99.5 × 83 cm
Widener Collection

Above
57 SIMON VOUET
Saint Jerome and the Angel
Canvas, 144.8 × 179.8 cm
Samuel H. Kress Collection

REMBRANDT VAN RIJN
The Apostle Paul
Plate 55

Holland in the seventeenth century was probably the most religiously tolerant European country, and many Jews fled there from religious persecution in Spain and Portugal. There was a substantial Jewish community in Amsterdam where Rembrandt lived, and he used to paint the rabbis and elders and observe their customs. It may be that there was a Jewish model for this painting of Saint Paul. Other paintings of Apostles are known, and perhaps Rembrandt intended to complete the full series. Saint Paul, although strictly not one of the original 12, is often added to the number. The saint has been represented as a scholar sitting in his study with heavy volumes piled on the table. He is lost in thought, possibly caught in the middle of one of his *Epistles* to the

early churches. To the right is the sword, his symbol of martyrdom. Dating from about the same period as the *Self-Portrait*, the brush strokes of the painting have been applied in an equally broad manner. Only the upper portion of the saint's face is in light, the lower part merging into the dark material of his gown. This emphasizes his intellectual preoccupation and perhaps signifies that as light comes from above, so the source of knowledge and truth lies in God. But if the colours are subdued, they are still warm, with patches of red in the Apostle's clothing, especially his left sleeve, and throughout the whole composition. Both the Widener and Mellon Collections are particularly rich in Rembrandt's paintings.

REMBRANDT VAN RIJN
Portrait of a Lady with an Ostrich-Feather Fan
Plate 56

This portrait, painted some time in the 1660s – the last digit of the date is not clear – indicates that not all of Rembrandt's fashionable clientèle had deserted him in his later years. The earrings, brooch, bracelets and rings in this painting are evidence that the lady was well-to-do. Rembrandt has not lingered on these exterior marks of wealth because he was more interested in his subject's face. She is not beautiful, but the strong light which reveals this, also discloses a sympathetic and intelligent countenance. The crossed hands, one so effortlessly holding the fan, are beautifully painted. They close the composition and at the same time give a feeling of restfulness. Rembrandt's ability to

create plastic forms with a few brush strokes is well demonstrated by the linen cuffs, which have an almost abstract quality, framing the hands. Much of our pleasure in the portrait derives from its formal composition. The upper section of the lady's dress, covered with a linen scarf, is in contrast to the dark lower area, and the straight line dividing the two also comes in the middle of the painting. By these subtle groupings of light and dark patches Rembrandt has created an imposing portrait of great dignity. The picture, together with its companion piece, a portrait of a man, once belonged to the Russian prince Félix Youssoupoff, who managed to bring them out of the country after the Revolution.

SIMON VOUET
Paris 1590 – 1649
Saint Jerome and the Angel
Plate 57

The influence of Caravaggio, who worked in Rome in the decades on either side of 1600, was immense, not only in Italy, but also in other places where artists appreciated his revolutionary style. His realism seemed like a breath of fresh air to younger painters after the artificial conventions of Mannerism. Vouet worked in Rome for several years, arriving there soon after Caravaggio's death, so it is not surprising that the older master's influence was still predominant. Later, Vouet was to change his style and become more restrained and classical, using cool, clear tones. But here, the influence of early Baroque painting is evident in the rhythm of the opposing gestures of the angel and Saint Jerome, and their contrasted heads. Light falls strongly on the

saint's face and body, and on part of the angel's swirling drapery, but the latter's face is in deep shadow. There are beautiful still-life passages in the convoluted cloth at the corner of the table and the various parts of the saint's writing equipment. Saint Jerome translated the Bible into Latin, but Vouet has not idealized the scholar in his study. He is painted as an old man with a wrinkled, troubled face, interrupted at his task by an angel urging him to complete it. The skull, hour-glass and other items on the table are reminders of human mortality and the need to hurry on with his translation. This painting once belonged to the Barberini family; Urban VIII, the head of the family, was Pope when Vouet worked in Rome.

58 · NICOLAS POUSSIN
The Baptism of Christ
Canvas 95.5 × 121 cm
Samuel H. Kress Collection

NICOLAS POUSSIN
Les Andelys 1594 – Rome 1665
The Baptism of Christ
Plate 58

Poussin was French by birth, but he spent most of his working life in Rome. There he found the twin inspirations for his art: antique sculpture and the classical paintings of Raphael. From these he created his own style in opposition to the Baroque then predominant in Italian art. Poussin almost worshipped the world of ancient Rome, and many of his paintings have subjects drawn from classical history or mythology. However, he could not ignore Christianity in the headquarters of the papacy; after all, church commissions provided most of the work for painters and sculptors. Nonetheless, Poussin gives his religious pictures a classical setting. The clothing, architecture and the objects have a strict archaeological accuracy. This almost pedantic attitude was characteristic of Poussin's later years. Earlier, a more lyrical quality is still discernible, and the modelling of the figures, as in *The Baptism*, is softer, and the colours less harsh than in his most doctrinaire paintings. Poussin's admiration for classical sculpture is evident in the nude men on the left, each in a different pose, while the figures are arranged in a frieze. Christ and the two figures on the right, who may be angels, are less sculptural and their faces are close to those in Raphael's paintings, especially the *Cartoons* and the Vatican frescoes. There is an almost direct quotation from Raphael's *School of Athens* in the gesticulating figures to the left of centre. *The Baptism* is part of a series of the Seven Sacraments, five remaining in an English private collection. They were commissioned by Cassiano dal Pozzo, Poussin's most important Roman patron, for whom he provided some of his most erudite painting. This was the last of the series to be completed and was finished in Paris where the painter had been summoned. A second, more classical, set of the Seven Sacraments, painted a few years later, survives entire in Scotland. Poussin's influence on French painting was strong and lasted into the eighteenth century.

72

59 CLAUDE LORRAIN
The Judgment of Paris
Canvas, 112.3 × 149.5 cm
Ailsa Mellon Bruce Fund

CLAUDE LORRAIN
Champagne 1600 – Rome 1682
The Judgment of Paris
Plate 59

Like Poussin, Claude lived much of his life in Rome. He was influenced by the countryside around, the *Campagna Romana*, so full of classical remains. Even more important was the profound effect of the German painter Elsheimer, a near contemporary, who also settled in Rome; his imaginative and evocative landscapes are foretastes on a smaller scale of what Claude later produced. He wanted to create classical landscapes based on an ideal past, rather than paintings concerned with the factual world of the present. The light is soft, often the golden light of sunset, which tinges his pictures with a haunting melancholy, as though longing for a long-lost age that can never be regained. Through the engravings after the *Liber Veritatis*, a record in drawings of his compositions, which includes this painting, Claude became known to a wide audience. His influence on later painters was considerable, especially in England, where he also inspired a new form of landscape gardening. *The Judgment of Paris* came from an English collection, having been lost sight of for over 200 years. Claude did not always paint his figures with the skill he devoted to landscape and sometimes he used the help of other artists. Here, the figures are exceptionally well painted and the scale is unusually large. The story of Paris is linked to the history of Troy; Paris' father, the king, had exiled him as an infant on account of an ill-omened prophecy. The god Hermes asked Paris to choose the most beautiful among the three goddesses: Hera, seen with her peacock; Minerva, who has laid aside her helmet and spear; and Aphrodite, attended by Eros. Paris gave the prize of beauty, appropriately, to Aphrodite, the goddess of love. This eventually brought about the Trojan War, but in this elegiac painting there is no indication of the fateful results of Paris' decision.

73

60 GEORGES DE LA TOUR
The Repentant Magdalen
Canvas, 113 × 92.7 cm
Ailsa Mellon Bruce Fund

GEORGES DE LA TOUR
Vic 1593 – Lunéville 1652
The Repentant Magdalen
Plate 60

We know very little about La Tour's life and where he was trained, but there is no doubt that the Caravaggesque school of Utrecht, and especially those who painted nocturnal subjects, were the major inspirations of his style. Lorraine during much of La Tour's lifetime was a battlefield fought over by the French and Imperialist forces. Callot has left a record of the brutalities suffered by the population. Perhaps these tribulations encouraged the religious revival, associated with La Tour's paintings, which took place then. The Magdalen, who is one of the outstanding types of Christian penitence and contemplation, was painted in several versions by La Tour. It is a natural choice for a subject in a period of religious fervour, particularly as the Counter-Reformation emphasized the sacrament of penance which the Protestants denied. Yet there is a classical calm far removed from

the extreme emotion of revivalism. All is silent and still, the only movement being the candle flame, and this tranquility must be associated with the strict Franciscan friars, the Capuchins, who were La Tour's friends and patrons. The Magdalen contemplates a skull, a long-established symbol of human mortality, but it is not the skull on the table that she regards, but the oblique reflection in the mirror, representing her past life. Her hand, almost translucent against the flame, stands out clearly against her strongly-lighted sleeve. The exact gradation of the candlelight falling on the Magdalen and the objects in front of her is an example of La Tour's technical mastery. In spite of having been famous and rich in his own day, La Tour was soon forgotten, and it was not until the twentieth century that he was rediscovered.

74

61 JAN VERMEER
Woman holding a Balance
Canvas, 42.5 × 38 cm
Widener Collection

JAN VERMEER
Delft 1632 – 1675
Woman Holding a Balance
Plate 61

In his observation and rendering of light no artist surpassed Vermeer; however, the appreciation of his paintings is a relatively modern phenomenon. Vermeer lived obscurely and became totally forgotten until the nineteenth century. When a painting of his entered the English Royal Collection in the eighteenth century, it was thought to be by van Mieris, a contemporary of Vermeer who was then much admired; the painting was criticized for its cold colouring and faulty style. Vermeer's total work numbers only about 40 paintings. He died in debt, leaving a widow and 11 children, so he probably had not made much money from painting. Today his pictures are highly prized and the National Gallery is fortunate in possessing four examples of his work. *Woman Holding a Balance* belongs to Vermeer's mature period when he had established complete mastery in his perception of light. The cool daylight falls evenly on the woman's face and the upper part of her clothing, suffusing them with a soft radiance. With incredible refinement Vermeer records the transition from highlight to shadow. The liquid drops of the pearl necklace and the gold on the table shine with a muted brilliance, so that the tonal values are evenly distributed. The setting is an ordinary interior, but the significance of what the woman is doing is underlined by the painting of *Christ in Judgment* on the wall, where the souls of men are being weighed in the balance to determine whether they will go to heaven or hell. As the woman is pregnant, Vermeer may be trying to symbolize life from the unborn to the Last Judgment – the span of man's existence.

LOUIS LE NAIN
Laon c 1593 — Paris 1648
A French Interior
Plate 62

Peasants in the seventeenth century were either laughed at for their boorish manners and ignorance or feared because of periodic violence. When they formed the subject matter of paintings it was usually the comical side that was stressed. Louis Le Nain, one of three artist brothers, was exceptional for the sympathy he brought to his paintings of peasants. The three main figures are meanly dressed, but they have a gravity and self-respect normally reserved for those higher in the social scale. There is a monumental quality in the woman, and the side figures, balancing each other, reinforce the composition's formality. It may be that Le Nain was thinking of a *Supper at Emmaus*, where the figures fall into a similar grouping, and the food and wine may be intended to have a religious significance. It could also be interpreted as grace before a meal. Each face expresses a different quality: the careworn yet handsome old man carrying a staff and bowl, perhaps symbolizing a pilgrim; the solid, comfortable-looking woman gazing directly at the viewer; the young boy already started on his life of toil. They might represent the three ages of man. Simple household goods, a pitcher, a glass, a pewter plate and the tub doing service as a table, all are as carefully painted as if they had been precious objects. Muted browns, fawns and greys, with the brightest colour the woman's russet jacket, give a unifying tonal scheme suitable to those working so close to the earth.

75

Above
62 LOUIS LE NAIN
A French Interior
Canvas, 55.6 × 64.7 cm
Samuel H. Kress Collection

Left
63 PHILIPPE DE CHAMPAIGNE
Omer Talon
Canvas, 225 × 161.6 cm
Samuel H. Kress Collection

PHILIPPE DE CHAMPAIGNE
Brussels 1602 – Paris 1674
Omer Talon
Plate 63

Working for the king, the queen and Cardinal Richelieu, Champaigne was at the centre of French political life in stirring times. When this portrait was painted, in 1649, Paris had rebelled against the crown. Omer Talon, the Attorney General of the *parlement* of Paris, strongly critized the government and defended his order's privileges against encroachment. The steadfast eyes and firm expression suggest his integrity and a determination to uphold justice. A concentration on the sitter's character and the classical presentation of him as the upright official, do not prevent Champaigne from following his Flemish inheritance of still-life naturalism in the clock, inkstand and book on the Turkish carpet covering the table, nor from contrasting the textures of the different materials. His early training with Poussin, and an intimacy with the austere Jansenist community at Port Royal, encouraged a restrained classicism in Champaigne. Everything is lucid and rational with simple, clear colouring. While an official portrait has some of the standard trappings of the grand style in the column and folds of drapery, they are not treated in a Baroque manner. Perhaps a more sensitive colourist might have chosen a shade of pink that harmonized better with Talon's robes, but for Champaigne the curtain was merely a backdrop to his subject's head which is the pivotal centre of the composition, and the artist has concentrated on making the head as expressive and forceful as possible.

JACOB VAN RUISDAEL
Haarlem c 1628 – Amsterdam 1682
Forest Scene
Plate 64

It may seem paradoxical that the largely flat countryside of Holland gave rise to the first major European school of landscape painting. The wide-open spaces and varying effects of light stimulated in painters a new emotional response to what had before been taken for granted. However, Ruisdael's paintings were not always based on his native Dutch scenery, and his introduction to the forests and mountains of Friesland and Germany which he saw on his travels, provided a stimulus to his imagination. These gave a more romantic quality to his paintings, the dark greens of the trees tinging them with melancholy. In this landscape the only figures are on a tiny scale, dwarfed by the immensity of nature. The dominant features in the composition are the river and waterfall, perhaps representing the course of human life. A dead tree with whitened limbs, standing dramatically in the foreground, may be another commentary on life's transitoriness. Ruisdael's pictures did not find much appreciation among contemporaries, but they came to be admired in the nineteenth century when their romantic feeling evoked an answering response and influenced the development of landscape painting. He is now regarded as the major Dutch landscapist of his time.

MEINDERT HOBBEMA
Amsterdam 1638 – 1709
A View on a High Road
Plate 65

In contrast to his master, Jacob van Ruisdael, Hobbema's landscapes are placid and without the intense emotional feeling of the older painter. Through the influence of his wife, who was the burgomaster of Amsterdam's cook, Hobbema became a minor customs official, and his painting career is often said to have terminated shortly afterwards. In fact, dated works of a later period are evidence that he did not stop painting completely on taking up his bureaucratic post. However, it is true that most of them fall within the decade of the 1660s; the present painting is dated 1665. The meandering road leading our eye into the composition, may seem no more than a cart track, but as most people walked or rode on horseback there was little need for better surfaces. The course of highroads wandered haphazardly, following the ancient paths and twisting to avoid trees and buildings. Some travellers are walking or riding watched by the local inhabitants. These figures are not by Hobbema but by another artist, and this practice, of using more than one artist for a painting, was common at the time. The three cottages in the middle distance, situated picturesquely among the trees, are placed on a diagonal to create further recession. A gap in the trees leads to a sunlit field and opens up a distant prospect, so that the view is not completely closed. Hobbema's restful landscapes were not much appreciated in his lifetime, but in the eighteenth and nineteenth centuries, especially in England, they became sought after. They had an influence on English painters such as Gainsborough and Constable.

Right
64 JACOB VAN RUISDAEL
Forest Scene
Canvas, 105.5 × 131 cm
Widener Collection

Right
65 MEINDERT HOBBEMA
A View on a High Road
Canvas, 93 × 128 cm
Andrew W. Mellon Collection

66 AELBERT CUYP
The Maas at Dordrecht
Canvas, 115 × 170 cm
Andrew W. Mellon Collection

AELBERT CUYP
Dordrecht 1620 – 1691
The Maas at Dordrecht
Plate 66

Although Cuyp came from a family of painters, he was comfortably off and painted for pleasure rather than as a professional. His works have frequently been forged and imitated, which is evidence of the esteem in which he was held. Cuyp lived all his life in Dordrecht and the town often appears in his landscapes. Here, it can be recognized on the left with the conspicuous fifteenth-century tower of the Groote Kerk in the background. Through the works of Jan Both, who had studied in Rome and come under the influence of Claude, Cuyp absorbed the mellow colouring of the Italianate school in Dutch painting. Yet instead of the *Campagna Romana*, it was the flat landscape of the Rhine and Maas estuaries that gave him all he needed to create pictures of intense poetry. Light floods his landscapes, giving them the silvery sheen of early morning, as in this view, or the warm glow of sunset. A low horizon allows him to leave much of the canvas as sky, and his clouds are not only painted with marvellous poetry, but are the result of careful observation. The English painter Turner, who was also fascinated by light,

created one of his masterpieces under the direct influence of Cuyp. It is not certain who is boarding the large passenger boat in the foreground, but he clearly was of some importance for he is being welcomed with drum and trumpet, a cannon fires a salute and the ships and river bank are crowded with people. The man wearing the large feathered hat has sometimes been identified with Charles II returning to England after exile in 1660. However, Cuyp is more concerned with recreating the river landscape than in recording any particular event. The long line of boats on the left, whose reflections in the water are so subtly observed, is used to create depth; and in addition to linear perspective, Cuyp employs atmospheric recession, making the furthest point the brightest. This happens to be just above the principal figure, who stands out against the light, and the eye is once more brought back to the foreground.

67 GERARD TER BORCH
The Suitor's Visit
Canvas, 80 × 75 cm
Andrew W. Mellon Collection

GERARD TER BORCH
Zwolle 1617 – 1681
The Suitor's Visit
Plate 67

Thanks to the many paintings of scenes from everyday life, we know a good deal about the houses, clothes and manners of the Netherlands in the seventeenth century, which was a period of great prosperity for the Dutch. They led Europe in trade, science and technology, and had successfully repulsed Spain, the mightiest land power of the day. Ter Borch himself was present at the Treaty of Münster in 1648, which ended the war with Spain, and painted a group portrait of the diplomats who signed the peace. The Dutch were full of self-confidence and proudly displayed their way of life before strangers. There is something immediately appealing in being able to look at a scene, such as the present painting, as if we were watching a play on the stage. While the traditional title was not provided by the artist, it is quite a plausible one. The glances exchanged between the elegantly dressed young man – the Dutch were noted for their

fine and spotless linen — and the woman in a red bodice are certainly full of meaning. The woman's is searching, as if she is sizing him up, while the suitor's, as befits his still ambivalent position, is more hesitant, uncertain of his reception. The young girl, the centre of the drama, ignores the visitor and concentrates on playing the theorbo, a kind of lute popular at the time, which appears frequently in paintings. Her father looks round from the fireplace where he is warming himself, no doubt having approved the visit. Marriages were usually arranged among the upper class, for, where property was involved, the question was too important to be settled on the basis of thoughtless passion. Ter Borch obviously delighted in painting rich stuffs, and has expressed with the greatest accuracy the different textures of silk in the women's dresses, the suitor's collar and cuffs, the green velvet of the chair and the Turkish carpet on the table.

GIUSEPPE MARIA CRESPI
Bologna 1665 – 1747
Lucretia Threatened by Tarquin
Plate 68

The neat division into centuries which historians are so fond of, does not take into account those whose careers span the arbitrary dividing line. Crespi is a case in point. He was an artist grounded in the Baroque tradition of the seventeenth century, but lived until the middle of the following century. He was influential, both in his subject matter and his style of strongly contrasted light and shade, on younger painters in his native Bologna, and also, through Piazzetta, on Tiepolo and Venetian painting. Crespi painted many religious pictures, but he was, too, an amused observer of the world around him. He produced a very personal kind of genre painting, usually based on life among the lower classes, which was very popular with his aristocratic patrons. In this painting, the subject is serious. The importance of female

virtue, however lightly some may regard it today, was never in doubt in eighteenth-century Italy nor in ancient Rome where the original tragedy took place. Lucretia, a girl of noble family, was raped by Tarquin, a member of the royal Etruscan house then ruling Rome. Unable to bear her disgrace, Lucretia stabbed herself and her brothers vowed to revenge her dishonour. The result set in motion a series of events which led to the expulsion of the alien dynasty. The story of Lucretia may be mythical or it may be true. For the Romans it represented the evils of tyranny, and for later ages the incident came to be regarded as the abuse of power on the helpless innocent. Crespi's normal colour scheme of brown and greys with dramatic chiaroscuro is particularly appropriate for this lurid drama.

NICOLAS DE LARGILLIÈRE
Paris 1656 – 1747
Elizabeth Throckmorton
Plate 69

Largillière studied in England and Flanders where he developed an admiration for van Dyck and the rich colouring and fluid brushwork of the Flemish school. His portraits span the long period of Louis XIV, the Régence and Louis XV, and retain the robust character of his early years. Elizabeth Throckmorton and her sisters were Dominican nuns, and all were painted in Paris in 1729 wearing their religious habits. The paintings, together with that of their brother, later 4th Baronet, were intended for English relatives and remained undivided at Coughton Court, Warwickshire, until recently. The Throckmortons belonged to an old recusant family who remained Roman Catholic in spite of persecution and social

discrimination. The penal laws, which prohibited them from sending their children abroad to be educated, were still in force, but by this time were rarely imposed. Largillière has used the black and white habit to good effect, the subject's veil falling symetrically on either side and framing her long, oval face. Elizabeth Throckmorton's features are sensitively treated and her nun's costume sets off her attractiveness. There is no feeling of resentment or sorrow at having to renounce the world, in her expression. While her religious vocation was doubtless sincere, girls of good family commonly entered convents if they had a small fortune and no likelihood of marrying, and these often aristocratic establishments guaranteed them a secure home for life.

Above
68 GIUSEPPE MARIA CRESPI
Lucretia Threatened by Tarquin
Canvas, 195 × 172 cm
Samuel H. Kress Collection

Top Right
69 NICOLAS DE LARGILLIÈRE
Elizabeth Throckmorton
Canvas, 81.3 × 65.7 cm
Ailsa Mellon Bruce Fund

Right
70 JEAN-BAPTISTE-SIMÉON CHARDIN
The Attentive Nurse
Canvas, 46.2 × 37 cm
Samuel H. Kress Collection

JEAN-BAPTISTE-SIMÉON CHARDIN
Paris 1699 – 1779
The Attentive Nurse
Plate 70

In spite of art theorists placing still-life painting very low in the hierarchy of subject matter, because it imitated real life rather than relying on imagination, Chardin's genius was acknowledged in official circles. When he exhibited in a public square in Paris, his work caused a sensation and he was elected to the Royal Academy, of which he eventually became treasurer. Chardin continued the tradition of seventeenth-century French and Dutch still-life painting. Sometimes the still-life objects make up the whole composition. At others, he incorporated them into a genre painting, as in this example, where the earthenware pots, the copper pan, jug, bread and other items on the table are integral parts of the picture. Chardin also depicted a side of French life not normally shown by painters: bourgeois domestic scenes treated without satire or condescension. He recorded with complete honesty, making no concessions to sentimentality or picturesqueness. Chardin usually painted directly on to the canvas. Sometimes he employs a thick impasto, a thick layering of colour; at others, scumbling, which allows another underlying colour to show through; or he uses delicate glazes. All are harmonized with a sure sense of tone, giving every part its due.

CANALETTO
Venice 1697 – 1768
View in Venice
Plate 71

Canaletto was the most famous painter of picture postcards in eighteenth-century Venice. His canvases portray a vivid image of contemporary Venetian life. Visitors on the Grand Tour brought these paintings back home as souvenirs of their stay in the city of pleasure. This is quite likely the origin of the present painting which came from an English collection. The particular view, which is of the Campo Ss. Giovanni e Paolo, with the church of the same name in the foreground, must have been popular, because several versions exist. In front of the church is Verrocchio's famous statue of *Colleoni*, and to the left is the Scuola di S. Marco, now a hospital. Architecturally, Venice has changed little since Canaletto's day. Certainly the present scene could be easily recognized by a modern tourist. Perhaps it is this feeling of *déjà vu* that gives Canaletto's paintings their widespread appeal. The compositions are generally treated as if the onlooker were observing a stage setting, a reflection of his early training as a theatre designer. They are accurately recorded, although Canaletto sometimes ignored changes to buildings, relying on his out-of-date drawings. For most of his life he painted his views in the studio, and later the figures were added with almost calligraphic brevity. Canaletto's early paintings of Venice have a spontaneous quality lacking in his later works which were repeated in response to tourist demand. This does not appear to have bothered his patrons, looking for a correct record of the city where they spent many enjoyable hours.

FRANCESCO GUARDI
Venice 1712 – 1793
Campo San Zanipolo
Plate 72

The view is the same as in Canaletto's painting, San Zanipolo being Venetian dialect for Ss. Giovanni e Paolo. Yet Guardi's treatment is clearly very different. He was notorious for the inaccuracy of his topography. Where Canaletto was happy to follow literally what he saw, making use of the mechanical assistance of a camera obscura, Guardi, with his greater imagination, wished to exercise artistic interpretation. His nervous style, with flecks of paint scattering colour and light throughout the composition, did not lend itself to accuracy. It so happens that Guardi's painting is one of his rare attempts to record a particular occasion. The view was probably taken on the spot as a sketch for a larger picture, one of four, commissioned by the Venetian government. The scenes illustrate the visit of Pope Pius VI in 1782. This event took place on the last day of the visit when the Pope blessed the faithful in the Campo. Guardi must have gone there soon afterwards because the temporary structure is still standing; the natural curiosity of the crowd can be seen in the people climbing up and down the stairs. Guardi has adopted a dark background to show up the spectators, who are composed in a few rapid brush strokes, and the patches of white, which dance across the canvas, lead the eye from figure to figure, giving a vivid animation to the scene.

Above
71 CANALETTO
View in Venice
Canvas, 71 × 112 cm
Widener Collection

Left
72 FRANCESCO GUARDI
Campo San Zanipolo
Canvas, 37.5 × 31.5 cm
Samuel H. Kress Collection

73 FRANÇOIS BOUCHER
Madame Bergeret
Canvas, 143 × 105 cm
Samuel H. Kress Collection

FRANÇOIS BOUCHER
Paris 1703 – 1770
Madame Bergeret
Plate 73

No century achieved such a high standard of civilization as the eighteenth, and life in France, for the upper classes at least, reached a degree of refinement never excelled. It was by keeping rude nature at a distance that such a level was maintained. After all, we now know how skin-deep is the veneer of civilization, so the eighteenth-century attitude must not be condemned as artificial. Nature was charming when it was tamed: neat lawns, clipped hedges and carefully planted groves were the nearest most Frenchmen, living in Paris or Versailles, ever came to seeing a natural landscape. They would have closed their eyes in horror at the wild mountains and moors admired by the Romantics. Boucher perfectly reflects this point of view; his landscapes are obviously imaginary, tenanted by beribboned sheep, handsome shepherds and shepherdesses and the most picturesque cottages, all totally removed from the dirt, ugliness and squalor of real peasant life. In the portrait of Madame Bergeret even the flowers look as if they were made of silk and velvet. She was clearly a charming person, and her death two years after Boucher painted her, came tragically early. She married a member of the *haute bourgeoisie*, a rich financier who was a patron of the arts. Her husband commissioned several works from Boucher. Madame Bergeret came from an artistic background; her grandfather had been court painter to Louis XIV, and her brother, the abbé Saint-Non had been taught by Boucher and was a patron of Hubert Robert and Boucher's pupil Fragonard.

74 JEAN-HONORÉ FRAGONARD
The Swing
Canvas, 215.9 × 185.5 cm
Samuel H. Kress Collection

JEAN-HONORÉ FRAGONARD
Grasse 1732 – Paris 1806
The Swing
Plate 74

It is impossible to appreciate the combination of elegance and comfort with which the upper classes were surrounded in eighteenth-century France. As Talleyrand said, only those who had lived before the French Revolution could appreciate the *douceurs de la vie*. Ladies and gentlemen devoted their whole lives to pleasure. No social consciousness disturbed them or made them aware that such leisure had to be based on the work of the vast majority of the population. This insouciance is widespread in the paintings of the period, beginning with Watteau's magical *fêtes galantes*. Heedless of the coming political storm they enjoyed themselves in innocent pastimes such as looking through a telescope, sitting on a swing, bathing the dog or chatting to friends, all of which we can observe in Fragonard's painting. The elegant park with its fountains and the balustrade keeping out the wilder landscape on the right, is typical of thousands near Paris

where the aristocracy and rich *bourgeoisie* spent the summers. Fragonard was particularly suited to paint this fantasy world. His light-hearted subjects, sometimes sentimental and with a frequently erotic tone, match the hedonistic society of eighteenth-century France. The landscape is always smiling and bathed in sunshine. The sparkling rococo brushwork in the trees, clouds and figures creates a wonderful feeling of gaiety and delight. Such a carefree attitude would doubtless be condemned by the killjoys and doctrinaire egalitarians of today, and the humourless leaders of the French Revolution had no time for Fragonard's art, so that he had to leave Paris and return to his native town; his last years were lived in poverty. But only a misanthrope could fail to respond to the charm and vitality of Fragonard's paintings. *The Swing* and its companion, *Blindman's Buff,* once belonged to the abbé Saint-Non, brother of Madame Bergeret.

75 FRAGONARD
A Girl Reading
Canvas, 81.1 × 64.8 cm
Gift of Mrs. Mellon Bruce

FRAGONARD
A Girl Reading
Plate 75

His often erotically explicit paintings might suggest that Fragonard was merely a contriver of pretty and titillating confections; but this was not so. No artist in eighteenth-century France exceeded Fragonard's control of paint. He was a master of conveying plastic form and his brushwork is always exciting. Observe how admirably he has represented the roundness of the girl's arm, and the tightness of her dress, her stomach and her bosom. The cushion also has an obviously tactile plumpness; we can almost feel the pressure where the girl is leaning against it. With bold strokes of yellow Fragonard highlights the dress hanging over the edge of the chair and creates an exciting pattern to follow. In the same way, the ruff with its meandering folds which are incised into the paint with the end of the brush, attracts our eye and provides the necessary break between the girl's head and her dress, also coming at a change of planes. A strong light from the left defines the form of the girl's head and body and her face is illuminated in sharp profile. It is not known who the sitter was or if the painting was a portrait. Whatever Fragonard's purpose, he has created a charming picture of innocent girlhood.

76 HUBERT ROBERT
The Old Bridge
Canvas, 91.3 × 121 cm
Samuel H. Kress Collection

HUBERT ROBERT
Paris 1733 – 1808
The Old Bridge
Plate 76

The classical past of Greece and Rome was still very important to cultivated men of the eighteenth century. Tourists journeyed to Italy to admire antique architecture and sculpture. Most of the buildings were in ruins, but were often extremely picturesque, with later additions stuck on and vegetation growing out of the stones. A taste for classical ruins, as well as those of other periods, encouraged landowners to build artificial ones in their parks. By endowing the past with a fictitious glamour this, in some ways, is a foretaste of the Romantic attitude to it. The ruins, real or false, evoked a pleasing melancholy, a nostalgia for a past which the spectator had never known and which had never existed. Robert, who had spent 11 years in Italy, came under the spell of Italian architecture and also felt the influence of the gardens in and around Rome. These he incorporated into his paintings. In this view of an old bridge he used the familiar Ponte Salario, a

Roman structure of the Republican period and partly destroyed during the barbarian invasions. In the Middle Ages a fortification had been constructed using some of the original stones; this in turn became a dwelling and, with the Italian genius for adaptation, it seems to be a natural element in the architecture. Robert added many picturesque details: the rugs hanging out to air, as they still do today; the vine-covered corner turret; the cow seen through the fence; and the young girls washing clothes in the river. The great arch of the bridge frames a beautiful landscape and introduces a dramatic note in the dark foreground contrasted with the light filled background. Such an idea may have come to Robert through the prints of his friend Piranesi.

77 GIOVANNI BATTISTA TIEPOLO
Apollo and Daphne
Canvas, 68.8 × 87.2 cm
Samuel H. Kress Collection

GIOVANNI BATTISTA TIEPOLO
Venice 1696 – Madrid 1770
Apollo and Daphne
Plate 77

The eighteenth century saw the last burst of creativity in Italian painting. Venice produced some of the finest artists of the period and Tiepolo concluded the splendid tradition of the sixteenth century. Tiepolo was directly linked to the earlier period through his admiration for Veronese, and he reproduced the cheerful colours and sumptuous details of the latter's paintings. Tiepolo's mastery was not confined to oil painting; he was a brilliant draughtsman, and many of his most inspired works were decorative and narrative frescoes. His fame took him outside Venice, and he journeyed to Würzburg and Madrid. Although he was a religious man and painted some deeply moving altarpieces, Tiepolo obviously felt at home in the world of classical mythology. The nymphs and goddesses gave him the chance to paint nudes, in which he excelled, and he has taken this opportunity with Daphne. She is about to turn into a laurel bush, her hands already sprouting leaves and twigs, and one foot a trunk, in answer to her prayer to be saved from the pursuit of Apollo. The man behind Daphne is her father, the river god Peneus, with his attributes of an oar and a jar. Cupid, who has caused all the mischief, is hiding behind Daphne's cloak. Apollo sees what is happening and realizes he has lost Daphne through his impetuosity. Tiepolo's palette, no doubt influenced by his frescoes, is high-toned and the paint is applied with bravura. The river god's red drapery makes a patch of brilliant colour, Apollo's cloak is appropriately gold, and Daphne's silver, and these bold colours are set against a resplendent blue background.

Left
78 VENETIAN SCHOOL
Before the Masked Ball
Canvas, 166.4 × 127 cm
Samuel H. Kress Collection

Above
79 GEORGE STUBBS
Colonel Pocklington with His Sisters
Canvas, 100.2 × 126.6 cm
Gift of Mrs Charles S. Carstairs

Right
80 SIR JOSHUA REYNOLDS
Lady Betty Hamilton
Canvas, 117 × 84 cm
Widener Collection

VENETIAN SCHOOL
Mid-eighteenth century
Before the Masked Ball
Plate 78

Sometimes a painting of high quality cannot be ascribed to a particular school. Whoever painted this picture was an extremely accomplished artist, and there are distinguishing characteristics in his style, notably the mannerisms of the hands, the large eyes he has given to his subjects and the scintillating treatment of the different stuffs, which should be enough to identify him. Nevertheless, although labelled Venetian, the painting has been attributed to artists ranging from France to Russia, and both Scandinavian and Polish origins have been suggested. The probable source is somewhere in the Austrian Empire where Latin, Slav and Teutonic cultures mixed so happily. The dominoes, or black masks, no doubt suggested a Venetian painter, but there is a strong central European influence in the subtle colouring and the architectural background. It may be the work of an expatriate Italian, then so much in demand in the artistically backward regions of Europe, but he remains unidentified. As the men are dressed in some kind of Hungarian costume and all carry masks, it is presumed that the subjects are going to a masquerade, so popular in the fashionable world at the time. The large scale suggests they might have been portraits, but we shall never know for certain.

GEORGE STUBBS
Liverpool 1724 – London 1806
Colonel Pocklington with His Sisters
Plate 79

Appreciation for Stubbs has come only in relatively recent years; he is now regarded as one of the greatest animal painters. He conducted detailed research into animal anatomies, spending many months in a lonely farmhouse patiently dissecting the bodies of horses and making exact drawings of what he saw. These Stubbs later engraved because he could find no one to do the work to his satisfaction. While best known for his horse paintings, Stubbs also painted other animals, both wild and domestic. Each is given the understanding and respect he gave to his human sitters. In this portrait of an officer in the Scots Guards, his two sisters and his horse, all are regarded as equally important, and the landscape has become an essential part of the composition, emphasizing the unity of nature. Stubbs' almost pantheistic attitude can be paralleled in the visionary painter and writer William Blake, and in the Lakeland poets Wordsworth and Coleridge. The English were among the first to respond emotionally to nature, just as they are still the leaders in the affectionate cult of animals.

SIR JOSHUA REYNOLDS
Plympton 1723 – London 1792
Lady Betty Hamilton
Plate 80

Until the eighteenth century there had been no proper school of English painting. Talented native artists certainly existed, but reliance was mainly on foreign painters. The tradition of importing artists from abroad began with Holbein and continued with van Dyck, Lely and Kneller, all of whom were predominantly portraitists. By the time Reynolds set up his studio in London the situation had altered. Hogarth had shown that it was not necessary to visit Italy or to ape foreign schools to produce an authentic English style of quality, and thanks largely to Reynolds himself, the prestige of English painting reached a European emminence. Reynolds became the undisputed leader of his profession, a position marked by his appointment as the first president of the Royal Academy. He was a learned man and moved in the literary world of Dr Johnson and his friends. The artists who had the most influence on Reynolds were van Dyck and the sixteenth-century Venetians who emphasized dashing brushwork and bright colour. When he painted under their inspiration he produced some of his finest work. *Lady Betty Hamilton* belongs to this category with the warm Venetian colouring in her dress. Reynolds was particularly good at painting children, putting them at their ease and avoiding sentimentality. Lady Betty's father was the Duke of Hamilton and she married the Earl of Derby. Through her unfaithfulness, the marriage broke down and the couple separated. There is no hint of this sad future in this appealing portrait of a five-year-old girl.

81 THOMAS GAINSBOROUGH
Landscape with a Bridge
Canvas, 113 × 133 cm
Andrew W. Mellon Collection

THOMAS GAINSBOROUGH
Sudbury 1727 – London 1788
Landscape with a Bridge
Plate 81

Like most English painters Gainsborough was a portraitist, but although he produced some of the most ravishing portraits of the whole century, his heart was not in them and he preferred landscapes. As he himself wrote; 'I'm sick of Portraits and wish very much to take my Viola-da Gamba and walk off to some sweet Village, where I can paint Landskips and enjoy the fag End of Life in quietness and peace.' Gainsborough is one of the founders of the English landscape school, which had such an effect on European sensibility in the period of Romanticism. However, his landscapes are not taken from actual views, nor generally from sketches made on the spot; they were in every sense fanciful. In his early years Gainsborough had been influenced by Dutch paintings of the seventeenth century which were plentiful in English collections. Later he turned to Rubens and his colours became warmer and more lyrical. Gainsborough's method of composition was peculiar. He brought into his painting room tree stumps, weeds, sand, pieces of coal or cork and looking glass which he placed on a table and arranged to form models for his landscapes. A contemporary records that Gainsborough 'would place cork or coal for his foregrounds, make middle grounds of sand or clay, bushes of mosses and lichens and set up distant woods of broccoli.' As the arrangements took place at night, the painter made dramatic use of artificial light. From the sketches he made up his finished paintings. Something of the broccoli-like quality in the trees may be attributed to this use of incongruous elements as a stimulus to his imagination. There is a never-never-land feeling in the landscape, enhanced by the unrealistic choice of colours, vibrant greens, blues and dove grey. This is a continuation of the Rococo tradition, but with a heightened emotional intensity. There are similarities with the backgrounds of Fragonard's paintings. Gainsborough's feathery brushwork, which gives such liveliness and poetry to his work, unites all the disparate elements and convinces us of the existence of his enchanted idyllic world.

82 BENJAMIN WEST
The Battle of La Hogue
Canvas, 152.7 × 214.3 cm
Andrew W. Mellon Fund

BENJAMIN WEST
Springfield, Pennsylvania 1738 – London 1820
The Battle of La Hogue
Plate 82

West was born in the American colonies, but he spent almost all his artistic life in England, where he became the favourite painter of George III and eventually succeeded Reynolds as president of the Royal Academy. He is therefore claimed by both the Americans and the British as one of their own. Nevertheless, with West the New World makes its bow on the stage of European painting. He had been to Rome in 1760, where incidentally he caused something of a sensation as the first American painter to visit there. At that time, *avant-garde* painters had turned away from the Rococo style to a reaffirmation of Classicism. West took these Neoclassical ideas to England and was one of the first to put them into practice. *The Battle of La*

Hogue is one of West's livelier paintings; his compositions, on good Neoclassical principles, tend to be static, even at times, wooden. He has captured the desperate hand-to-hand struggle, as with the pair in the water on the right; and there is a fine group of an English officer in a red feathered hat grasping the blue coat of a Frenchman clinging to a mast. All is confusion, noise and smoke and it must have been difficult to tell friend from enemy. The battle took place in 1692 when a French invasion attempt was defeated by the combined British and Dutch fleets. Such stirring history still lived on in patriotic memory, for in the eighteenth century the British and the French were continually at war.

83 JOHN SINGLETON COPLEY
Watson and the Shark
Canvas, 182.1 × 229.7 cm
Ferdinand Lammot Belin Fund

JOHN SINGLETON COPLEY
Boston, Massachusetts 1738 – London 1815
Watson and the Shark
Plate 83

The event commemorated in this painting took place in Havana harbour in 1749. The unfortunate protagonist, Brooke Watson, was attacked by a shark while swimming and lost a leg. He survived the ordeal and prospered, finally becoming Lord Mayor of London. He commissioned Copley to record the incident and the dramatic subject helped to establish the artist's reputation when the painting was exhibited at the Royal Academy. Copley had begun his career in Boston, Massachusetts, where he established a flourishing portrait practice. The political troubles in America forced him to leave, and he settled in London. It is easy to understand why Copley's

painting made a sensation. He had no need to add to the foreground drama through Baroque histrionics. The horror on the faces of the onlookers is genuine enough, and so is their determination to rescue the young man. It has the matter of fact quality of a piece of pictorial journalism. This realistic approach must be the result of Copley's lack of formal training in traditional history painting, which gives a directness to his style. Yet the years Copley had spent in Italy had not been wasted, for the figure of Watson is based on a piece of classical sculpture. Copley's apparent artlessness conceals a carefully planned composition.

GILBERT STUART
North Kingston, Rhode Island 1755 – Boston, Massachusetts 1828
Mrs Richard Yates
Plate 84

Like his fellow Americans West and Copley, Stuart went to work in England, where he stayed for over ten years. His extravagance and debts forced him to go to Ireland, and after five years there he had once more to flee his creditors and return to the United States. There he quickly established a flourishing practice, and Washington, Jefferson, Adams and other leaders of the young republic sat for their portraits. Thanks probably to letters of introduction from Irish friends, Stuart met Mrs Yates and her husband, a New York merchant whose portrait is also in the National Gallery, and painted several members of their family. The tradition of American painting was rather different from that which Stuart had known in the British Isles. Flattery and anything approaching the grand manner would have been out of place in a republican and democratic society. Mrs Yates, plainly dressed and wearing a somewhat dowdy cap, is very much the middle class housewife engaged at her sewing, which we can be sure was of a more practical kind than that which occupied fine English ladies. She looks almost annoyed at the interruption. Stuart has not made her a beauty, for she has an ugly masculine mouth and an inordinately long nose, but the artist has tactfully concealed her squint by making her look out of the corner of her eyes. The paint is applied with vigorous brush strokes, especially in the highlights, and here again Stuart modified his style from the softer painting of his earlier portraits. The result is an increased strength and conviction, and this portrait is one of Stuart's masterpieces.

FRANCISCO GOYA
Fuendetodos 1746 – Bordeaux 1828
The Marquesa de Pontejos
Plate 85

Although Goya continued working into old age, and many of his most important and original works belong to the nineteenth century, he lived mostly in the preceding century, in which he has been included. He had already established his reputation well before the French invasion of Spain, becoming a leading official of the Royal Academy and chief painter to the king. The marquesa is clearly a lady of the *ancien régime* as she stands rather stiffly, like a mechanical doll, with a carnation in her hand. Her costume is apparently simple, but must have been expensive for it is based on the shepherdess fashion worn by Marie-Antoinette. Her piled-up hair and the halo of the straw hat make her face seem small in comparison. Goya has concentrated on the externals, on the lady's pretty dress with all its ribbons and flowers, producing a wonderful symphony of silver-grey and pink. Yet there is curiously little life in the lady's face, which is like a mask concealing her emotion. The little dog is more animated than his mistress. Did she not have any feelings, or was Goya not interested in them? Perhaps for his fashionable clients he observed the convention, prevalent in eighteenth-century Europe, that well bred people did not show emotion. Goya certainly showed no such reticence in his portraits of the Spanish royal family. A certain reminder of Gainsborough's paintings in the composition can be explained by Goya's knowledge of English portrait engravings. The marquesa was married to the brother of Count Floridablanca, the chief minister to Charles III of Spain, and one of Goya's patrons.

GOYA
Señora Sabasa García
Plate 86

We are not only in a new century with this portrait, but confronted by a very different style. Instead of a verdant park there is a plain, dark background and the colour scheme is subdued: yellow-brown and white. Yet the figure stands out clearly. The ripples of the lady's shawl, passing over her shoulder, are painted with masterly observation. In her pale face, offset by brown ringlets, there is an intelligent expression, even if one feels the eyes and mouth conceal pent up emotion. Goya is supposed to have seen the subject as a girl of 18, and he was so struck with her charm that he asked to paint her portrait. The girl's uncle was a prominent Liberal politician who later became Spanish prime minister. Goya, like most of the Liberals, at first welcomed the French invasion which occurred soon after this portrait was painted because they hoped it would introduce reforms into Spain. The Royalist Restoration left him politically alienated, and this together with his deafness caused by a severe illness, made Goya introspective and he channelled his criticism into enigmatic paintings and etchings.

84 GILBERT STUART
Mrs Richard Yates
Canvas, 76.9 × 63.5 cm
Andrew W. Mellon Collection

97

86 GOYA
Señora Sabasa García
Canvas, 71 × 58 cm
Andrew W. Mellon Collection

85 FRANCISCO GOYA
The Marquesa de Pontejos
Canvas, 211 × 126 cm
Andrew W. Mellon Collection

87 JOSEPH MALLORD WILLIAM TURNER
Keelmen Heaving in Coals by Moonlight
Canvas, 92.3 × 122.8 cm
Widener Collection

JOSEPH MALLORD WILLIAM TURNER
London 1775 – 1851
Keelmen Heaving in Coals by Moonlight
Plate 87

With Turner, the English at last produced a painter of the first importance whose impact was felt outside his own country. His style both in water colours and oils changed greatly in a working life of nearly 60 years, as he came under the influence of different artists or responded to the scenery he saw on his continental tours. Turner loved the sea, and some of his finest paintings have it as the subject in all its variable moods. Light remained Turner's chief interest: how to convey luminosity through the medium of oil and water-colour. His visits to Venice were of crucial importance in this development. The peculiar lighting effects created by its situation — half land, half water — inspired Turner to capture this evanescence, first in his water-colours and then in his oil paintings, through using a white ground to heighten the tone. In this night scene of the colliers being loaded on the river, Turner exploited the different sources of light, natural or man made, giving each its proper intensity and contrasting its warm or cool properties. First there is the full moon shining through the haze, which irradiates the composition and confers a magic aura

on what must have been a drab scene. The reflection in the water makes the foreground as light as the sky and adds to the luminosity. The second main source of light comes from the orange flares of the colliers and the blast furnaces in the background, preventing the tones from being too cold. Thus even industrial activity can be tinged with romance. The black hulls on the right provide a dramatic contrast, silhouetted against the flares. With a few deft strokes Turner has sketched in the masts and rigging of the ships which act as coulisses to lead our eye in towards the centre. That space is left empty, the buoys and rafts being kept to the sides so that nothing can impede the core of light leading into the distance, which is the nub of the composition. An admiring critic wrote: 'And such a night! a flood of glorious moon-light wasted upon dingy coal-whippers, instead of conducting lovers to the appointed bower.'

99

88 JOHN CONSTABLE
Wivenhoe Park, Essex
Canvas, 56.1 × 101.2 cm
Widener Collection

JOHN CONSTABLE
East Bergholt 1776 – London 1837
Wivenhoe Park, Essex
Plate 88

Our manner of looking at the English countryside owes much to Constable. Unlike Turner, who drew on Switzerland and Italy for inspiration, Constable found all he needed in England. Indeed, even there, Constable's landscapes are mainly of the Essex-Suffolk border, where he was born, and of Salisbury and Hampstead, where he lived. These were sufficient subjects to allow him to express his deeply emotional response to nature. Constable made rapid small sketches on the spot, often recording the time of day and the weather, which he knew had such an effect on the varying moods of landscape. His acute and understanding observation of nature was unsurpassed, although when he came to paint in the studio he found difficulty, as he said, in recreating the 'feel of the landscape.' This is certainly not the case with *Wivenhoe Park*, which is the epitome of the English countryside. The lush green meadows contrast with the darker foliage of the trees, while the passing clouds, with their dappled shadows, give variety and contrast to the sky and the ground. The tranquil atmosphere is established by the cows placidly eating grass, and there are charming details attracting the eye to different parts of the landscape. Two boys are fishing in the lake; more children are playing on the bank to the right; and the young daughter of General Rebow, who commissioned the painting, is driving a donkey cart on the left. This was an addition Constable painted after he had completed the major part of the composition. In order to make his view more inclusive he added small strips on either side of the painting. From letters to his fiancée we know that Constable made many sketches in the open air at Wivenhoe. This freshness has been preserved in the finished painting, which is the quintessence of an English summer's day.

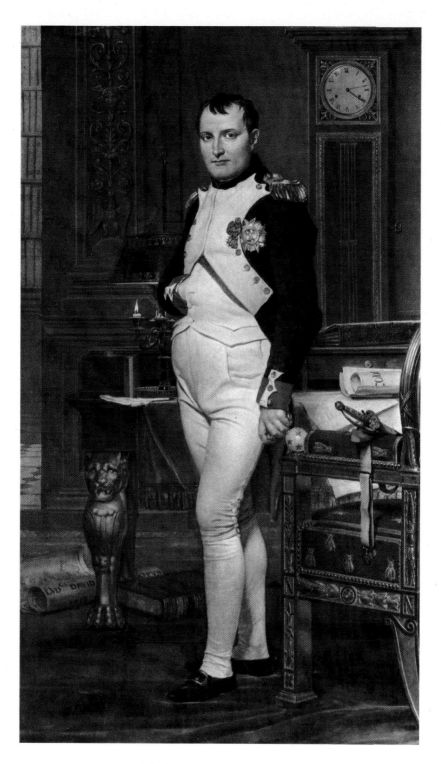

89 JACQUES-LOUIS DAVID
Napoleon in His Study
Canvas, 203.9 × 125.1 cm
Samuel H. Kress Collection

JACQUES-LOUIS DAVID
Paris 1748 – Brussels 1825
Napoleon in His Study
Plate 89

Napoleon was in many ways the forerunner of a modern dictator who fully appreciated the value of propaganda in the service of the state and his régime. David provided this, as he had already done for the French Revolution, but however fascinating these works may be as historical documents, paintings such as the huge *Coronation of Napoleon* lack the idealistic fervour of his earlier canvases. The relatively simple portrait of Napoleon is successful both as art and public relations, because it is understated. Here is the ruler and lawgiver working hard into the night at his desk, littered with papers, to provide good government for France and the Empire. He is prepared to forgo sleep for the common good: the clock shows it is after four o'clock and the candles are guttering. The sword has been laid aside for the pen, the

philosopher has taken the place of the warrior. Napoleon liked David's portrait because it provided the image he wanted. 'You have understood me, my dear David. By night I work for the well-being of my subjects and by day for their glory.' There is no reason to suppose that either the painter or his master doubted the truth of this pictorial statement. The sumptuous furnishings are in the Empire style, created to reflect the new glories of his rule, for all the arts had to be pressed into service to further Napoleon's prestige. The Napoleonic bees on the chair have replaced the Bourbon lilies. In contrast to these rich surroundings, Napoleon is simply dressed in uniform with only the Legion of Honour as a mark of distinction. The portrait was commissioned by a Scottish nobleman who admired Napoleon.

THÉODORE GÉRICAULT
Rouen 1791 – Paris 1824
Trumpeters of Napoleon's Imperial Guard
Plate 90

The greatness of Napoleon cast a spell on his age, and many people were caught up in the glories of his achievements as a general and as a ruler. Géricault was one of these and painted several pictures of Napoleonic soldiers. This group of trumpeters, resplendent in their scarlet and gold uniforms, belong to the Second Regiment of Light Horse Lancers of the Guard, and dates from around 1812–1814, when Napoleon's Empire disintegrated. The riders on their grey horses seem to be emerging from some dense fog which gives them a mysterious quality. They are painted with the freedom and spontaneity of a sketch. Horses

were Géricault's particular love and they appear in most of his paintings. He almost certainly brought about his own death because he insisted on riding when he was ill. Géricault is often regarded as an arch-romantic, and his dandyism, espousal of Liberal causes such as Greek independence and the abolition of slavery, an unhappy love affair and a career cut short in its prime, have all the ingredients of a Byronic hero. Yet, although the impact of Géricault's life was considerable, much more important was the influence of his limited output, for he pointed the way to much of later Romantic art and was admired by Delacroix.

Right
90 THÉODORE GÉRICAULT
Trumpeters of Napoleon's Imperial Guard
Canvas, 60.4 × 49.6 cm
Chester Dale Fund

91　JEAN·AUGUSTE·DOMINIQUE INGRES
Madame Moitessier
Canvas, 146.7 × 100.3 cm
Samuel H. Kress Collection

JEAN·AUGUSTE·DOMINIQUE INGRES
Montauban 1780 – Paris 1867
Madame Moitessier
Plate 91

Ingres studied under David, the leader of French Neoclassicism, and his years in Italy merely reinforced his devotion to the models of that style and in particular to Raphael and antique sculpture. He became in his turn the chief Neoclassical painter in France and continued faithful to the style long after it had gone out of fashion. For Ingres line was of supreme importance and colour very subordinate. His historical paintings, on which he placed such store, are not now as much admired as his portraits which Ingres professed to dislike. They rank among the finest in European painting. Perhaps the most appealing are the small pencil drawings done in Rome early in his career which possess a wonderful freshness, making some of his later work seem laboured. Ingres always complained about having to paint portraits, and it took years to complete the sittings for *Madame Moitessier*. She was in fact painted twice by Ingres, the

other portrait being in the National Gallery, London. Her simple black dress sets off the pearly whiteness of her arms and shoulders and complements the rich, purple wallpaper behind her. The lady's features are of the classical type favoured by Ingres with a small mouth and straight nose, and the statuesque frontal pose and hair parted in the middle, give her a formal symmetry. Ingres has not forgotten that she is a fashionable lady. The elaborate bracelets, which Ingres told her to bring to the sittings, and the roses in her hair, introduce a note of frivolity to relieve her severe expression.

92 EUGÈNE DELACROIX
Arabs Skirmishing in the Mountains
Canvas, 92.5 × 74.6 cm
Chester Dale Fund

EUGÈNE DELACROIX
Charenton Saint-Maurice 1798 – Paris 1863
Arabs Skirmishing in the Mountains
Plate 92

Both Ingres and Delacroix painted exotic subjects. Their treatment of them could not have been more different, for they were the leaders of two rival factions among painters, the Classicists and the Romantics. Ingres' Turkish odalisques might be made of marble and the erotic element is severely restricted. It cannot be coincidental that he had no first-hand knowledge of the East. Delacroix was strongly influenced by his direct experience of the Arab world when he travelled in North Africa. Scenes of the bazaar and the harem were calculated to appeal to him through their colourful activity. Delacroix's Arab women have all the fire and passion of their originals. Even at the end of his life, over 30 years after his visit, he painted this scene of Arabs fighting as if he had just witnessed the incident. The glowing colours, especially the predominant use of red and white with a brilliant blue sky, are the essence of Delacroix's style. So too is his exciting brushwork with the accents of light on the white clothing attracting the eye hither and thither. In contrast to the simple outlines of classicism, Delacroix's figures are complex. This can be seen in the dead horseman in the foreground and the almost mannered pose of the man to his right where every limb is on a different axis. Similarly, in the overall composition, there is a broad zigzag from the fallen horse and rider to the trees, then back to the fortress, and finally returning again to the hills on the right. Like Géricault, Delacroix loved to paint horses. There is more pathos in the struggle of the stricken horse than in the body of his dead master.

THOMAS COLE
Bolton-le-Moors, Lancashire 1801 – Catskill, New York 1848
The Voyage of Life: Youth
Plate 93

The beauties of their native landscape inspired the Hudson River school of painters, under Cole's leadership, to depict the untamed grandeur of America. While Cole made sketches on the spot, he used these in his studio for his romantic and imaginative paintings. This, the second version of *The Voyage of Life*, was painted in Italy. The small scale of his figures in relation to their architectural or, in the present case, natural background, which is common in Cole's work, derives from his knowledge of the engravings of the English artist, John Martin, then popular in America because of their exceptionally dramatic presentation of religious subjects. In an age and a country where Bunyan's *Pilgrim's Progress* was still one of the most read books, it came naturally to adopt the allegory of a voyage down the river of life to represent the span of man's existence. *Youth* is the second part of a series of four. In the clear noonday light the confident young man steers his ship without the aid of his guardian angel. The vision in the sky, looking like a celestial birthday cake, is, in the painter's words, an 'air built Castle . . . emblematic of the day-dreams of youth, its aspirations after glory and fame.'

JEAN-BAPTISTE-CAMILLE COROT
Paris 1796 – 1875
Landscape near Volterra
Plate 94

There is a marked contrast between Corot's early landscapes, influenced by his stay in Italy, and the vaporous tones and sketchy brushwork of his popular later paintings. This view in Tuscany, near Volterra, was exhibited in the *salon* of 1838 and was critized for being painted in a spiritless manner, and for its coldness and lack of brilliance. No doubt such adverse criticism was caused by Corot's refusal to comply with contemporary taste by providing anecdotal or sentimental details. He recorded the landscape directly as he saw it. Yet obviously the painting was not done on the spot, but recollected later with the aid of sketches he had made. Corot distilled his emotional response to the landscape so that the spectator shares his feelings. To do this he has carefully constructed the view, giving our eye ample time to sweep over the broad foreground, littered with rocks, until it follows the meandering path into the wood. The landscape is almost deserted and even the solitary horseman has his back to us so that nothing distracts from the contemplation of nature. Using the strong effects of light and shadow associated with Italy, Corot has created dramatic contrasts in the composition. The valley on the left is in deep shadow, but the distant prospect is bathed in sunshine. The foreground is also in shade, as is the wood with its welcoming coolness, but the horseman on his white horse, which is the brightest part of the painting, is surrounded by sunshine. But with all these contrasts there is a tonal harmony and structural unity in the tradition of Poussin, another French painter influenced by Italian landscape.

93 THOMAS COLE
The Voyage of Life: Youth
Canvas, 134.3 × 194.9 cm
Ailsa Mellon Bruce Fund

94 JEAN-BAPTISTE-CAMILLE COROT
Landscape near Volterra
Canvas, 69.5 × 95.1 cm
Chester Dale Collection

HONORÉ DAUMIER
Marseilles 1808 – Valmondois 1879
Advice to a Young Artist
Plate 95

There have been few satirists more biting than Daumier; the greed, corruption and hypocrisy of France under Louis-Philippe are forever recorded in his caricatures. Daumier was a journalist and produced several thousand lithographs which brought his satire to a wide audience. It also displeased the government, which attempted to suppress Daumier through imprisonment. He never idealized the working classes, however much he might have sympathized with them. Something of his rapid technique as a draughtsman can be found in his oil paintings where the nervous brushwork often has a calligraphic quality, as if he were using a pen. His colours are sombre, reflecting his view of life, for he had few ideals about man's virtue or altruism. Ironically, he was himself the recipient of kindness from Corot who had bought him a house when he had become almost blind and was very poor. This painting was a present to Corot in gratitude. The strongly-lighted heads are against a dark wall; the light also concentrates on the drawings which are the centre of interest. The composition has strong horizontals and verticals, the red couch balancing the two upright figures, and these opposites are echoed in the picture frames.

95 HONORÉ DAUMIER
Advice to a Young Artist
Canvas, 41 × 33 cm
Gift of Duncan Phillips

109

96 EDOUARD MANET
Gare Saint-Lazare
Canvas, 93.3 × 114.5 cm
Gift of Horace Havermeyer

EDOUARD MANET
Paris 1832 – 1883
Gare Saint-Lazare
Plate 96

Manet's early paintings are marked by their strong contrasts of light and shadow, his frequent use of black areas and his admiration for Hals, Velázquez and Goya who also influenced his free and liquid brushwork. Because his paintings were often rejected by the academic artists who formed the *salon*, he took part in the *Salon des Réfusés* in 1863 where he met kindred spirits in rebellion against the artistic *status quo*. Manet is usually called an Impressionist, but he would have refused the label and resented being associated with them in the public mind, for he craved official recognition and academic respectability. But the Impressionists certainly influenced his style by lightening his colours and making his painting even more fluid. He never gave up his use of black which, by contrast, gives greater brilliance to the other tones. The black railings through which the girl is looking serve this purpose, they also provide a necessary transition between the foreground figures and the steam of the locomotives, which would otherwise be difficult to place. Nineteenth-century painters such as Turner, used steam-engines as subjects, not only because they represented modernity and speed, but because they provided evanescent light effects as steam melted into air. Manet's incomparable use of paint, which he here applied directly on to the canvas, working out of doors in a friend's garden, is particularly evident in the girl's dress and the open book. His subtle colour sense adds small touches of red throughout the picture to relieve the dominant blue and white.

97 MANET
The Old Musician
Canvas, 187.4 × 248.3 cm
Chester Dale Collection

MANET
The Old Musician
Plate 97

At the time he painted this enigmatic work Manet was greatly influenced by seventeenth-century Spanish art, which had been revealed to his contemporaries through the collection of King Louis-Philippe. True to his belief that a new style had to be evolved by studying the Old Masters and applying their lessons to modern life, Manet based the composition on a painting by Velázquez which he knew from a print. The old man is derived from a peasant group by Le Nain, while the two boys refer back to Watteau and Ribera. Manet copied two of his own compositions in the girl holding the baby, which appeared in a painting two years before, and the man in the cloak is his famous *Absinthe Drinker*. All these disparate elements are harmonized by Manet's fluid brushwork and strong plastic treatment of the human form. Courbet would have used such a subject to convey a social message. Manet, however, was concerned with the handling of paint and surface texture.

98 HENRI FANTIN-LA TOUR
Portrait of Sonia
Canvas, 109.2 × 81 cm
Chester Dale Collection

HENRI FANTIN-LATOUR
Grenoble 1836 – Buré, Orne 1904
Portrait of Sonia
Plate 98

In addition to his well-known flower and still-life paintings, Fantin-Latour also produced portraits of distinction. The influence of photography, which interested so many nineteenth-century painters, is evident in the portrait of his niece Sonia, which has the form of the fashionable *carte de visite*. Because of the long exposure necessary for a photograph, the sitter had to remain very still and this has been transferred to the painting in the pronounced clarity of the face. The strong lighting then required for photography relentlessly exposes the individual features, with almost no half light to modify its harshness. At the same time, every detail of the ostrich feathers in the hat and the boa, and the individual strands in Sonia's fringe have been painted with exact care. The colours are low key to simulate the brown tonality of a daguerreotype. Yet the portrait is no mere mechanical exercise in painting virtuosity. It is an objective, but also sympathetic study of someone who must, from the inscription 'to my dear niece', have been close to the painter's affections.

CLAUDE MONET
Paris 1840 – Giverny 1926
Palazzo da Mula, Venice
Plate 99

'Only an eye, but my God what an eye!' Cézanne is supposed to have said of Monet. Certainly Monet, the leader of the Impressionists, pursued their ideals of recording exactly what the eye sees through an analysis of tone and colour. The Impressionists were concerned with the visible surface, with light playing on the many facets of an object, but they were not interested in the underlying reality. They used bright colours to intensify their vision, even in shadows, which through contemporary scientific research they knew to contain an object's complementary colour. Wishing also to record the fleeting moment in emulation of the camera, the Impressionists adopted a technique of small brush strokes to give a shimmering effect. This, and the exaggerated brightness of their colours, aroused intense opposition. Today it is difficult to understand what all the fuss was about, their ideas have become so incorporated in standard orthodoxy and their popularity exceeds all other schools. Monet has chosen to paint a Venetian canal at dusk when a blue-violet light plays across the buildings. Venice offered good opportunities to him for putting into practice Impressionist ideas. Its constantly changing light and sparkling surfaces, reflected from the water, were the epitome of an Impressionist composition. Monet's attitude to what he painted differed from that of another visitor to Venice, Turner. The latter was emotionally involved in his visionary recreation of what he had seen. Monet is more objective, but his amazing perception has changed our way of looking at the most familiar views.

AUGUSTE RENOIR
Limoges 1841 – Cagnes 1919
A Girl with a Watering Can
Plate 100

Renoir is one of the most important and probably the best loved of the Impressionist painters, but he went on later to develop his own personal way of painting based on his study of the Old Masters, whom he admired. His early training as a porcelain decorator attracted him to eighteenth-century French paintings, and their charm encouraged his predilection for pretty women and children as subjects. This enchanting little girl has obvious appeal and she is one of the favourites in the National Gallery. Renoir caught her still, for a moment, as if he had snapped a photograph. She is dressed in the rich blue which the painter liked using in his early period as it gave greater luminosity to the flesh tones. In the same way, he has given her a red bow and put red flowers in the background to provide the complementary colour of the grass, according to Impressionist principles. Renoir painted the little girl in the garden of his friend Paul Bérard. She may be one of Bérard's daughters. Thanks to the recent bequest of Mrs Mellon Bruce the National Gallery now owns over 40 paintings by Renoir.

Above
99 CLAUDE MONET
Palazzo da Mula, Venice
Canvas, 62 × 81.1 cm
Chester Dale Collection

Left
100 AUGUSTE RENOIR
A Girl with a Watering Can
Canvas, 100.3 × 73.2 cm
Chester Dale Collection

101 EDGAR HILAIRE-GERMAIN DEGAS
Mademoiselle Malo
Canvas, 81.1 × 65.1 cm
Chester Dale Collection

EDGAR HILAIRE-GERMAIN DEGAS
Paris 1834 – 1917
Mademoiselle Malo
Plate 101

His admiration for Ingres might have made Degas an academic painter, but the influence of Manet and the Impressionists changed his style. Degas became the main organizer of the Impressionist exhibitions. Because he was of independent means, he could afford to ignore public ridicule and painted the subjects of his choice: the grisettes, actresses and dancers of Paris. This also allowed him to experiment with various techniques, and he mastered several different methods in painting and graphics. Degas was a splendid portraitist and the Gallery has seven fine examples. Mademoiselle Malo danced in the ballet and was a friend of Degas. She is supposed to have been the mistress of the painter Tissot. For personal reasons, Degas kept this portrait until he died. Her face is painted with sensitivity and the tonal value is increased by her contrasting dark dress. The chrysanthemums behind her are treated as if they were a piece of material; this device of flattening the background comes from Japanese prints, which Degas, along with many of the Impressionists, admired. The sitter's informal pose has been influenced by photography which attracted painters because of the new compositional ideas it gave.

102 DEGAS
Four Dancers
Canvas, 151.1 × 180.2 cm
Chester Dale Collection

DEGAS
Four Dancers
Plate 102

With advancing years Degas' eye sight grew worse and, as a result, he was unable to paint as he had done earlier. Line began to give way to colour. He became preoccupied with what he held to be the secrets of the sixteenth-century Venetians, those supreme masters of colour. Mistakenly believing that Mantegna had used the technique, he adopted green underpainting with orange and yellow over it to give an interweaving of cool and warm tones. Degas also experimented with different media. Although this is in oil it has the freedom and broad brushwork of gouache or pastel with their heightened colour. Ballet had been one of the most constant themes in Degas' work, not only performances on the stage, but also the hours of tedious rehearsal which the audience never saw. Here, four ballerinas wait for their entrance in the wings. In spite of his failing vision, Degas remained a master of line. The heads and torsos of the dancers are drawn with sureness; their arms forming an intricate pattern and linking the figures to each other. In contrast, the skirts are loosely painted to convey the gossamer lightness of the material and in the similarly treated scenery, colour defines the form.

103 MARY CASSATT
Girl Arranging Her Hair
Canvas, 75 × 62.5 cm
Chester Dale Collection

MARY CASSATT
Pittsburgh, Pennsylvania 1845 – Le Mesnil-Théribus 1926
Girl Arranging Her Hair
Plate 103

It was considered hardly respectable for a well-born girl in the nineteenth century to study art where she might encounter unsuitable people and improper subjects. Mary Cassatt, the daughter of a Pittsburgh banker, must have been remarkably determined when she asserted her independence, travelled in Europe and eventually settled in Paris to paint. She became interested in the Impressionists and was invited to show her work at their exhibitions. Through her, Americans came to know Impressionist paintings and she encouraged her friends to buy them. Like many of her fellow artists, Mary Cassatt admired Japanese prints and her coloured aquatints, which are of a high quality, reflect this interest. Her paintings usually have feminine subjects: mothers and children or women chatting over the teacups. The theme of a girl combing or arranging her hair was often used by Degas, and Cassatt deliberately adopted it because he had challenged her to produce a work of real artistic merit. Degas felt that women were not capable of doing this, but the result proved him wrong and he acknowledged his error by buying the painting. Cassatt made her model unattractive and concentrated on the formal qualities. By bringing the figure to the foreground she creates a sense of immediacy, and she has reduced the background through the patterned wallpaper and minimized the washstand so that we can concentrate on the main figure.

104 ARNOLD BÖCKLIN
The Sanctuary of Hercules
Wood, 112 × 180 cm
Andrew W. Mellon Fund

ARNOLD BÖCKLIN
Basel 1827 – San Domenico di Fiesole 1901
The Sanctuary of Hercules
Plate 104

The dominance of French nineteenth-century painting has overshadowed other European schools and made them, until recently, unjustly neglected. The German-speaking countries produced many important painters, but because most of their work is in German or Swiss collections, they are hardly represented elsewhere. There were both strong classical and romantic strains in Germanic painting and Böcklin combines the two. He lived in Italy for long periods and had a profound knowledge of classical culture. Archaeological discoveries in Greece at the time Böcklin painted his picture, revealed the civilization of Homeric days, and the artist has shown his awareness of this in the roughly-hewn stones on the right. We are to suppose these the foundations of an ancient sanctuary on which

the more finished masonry of later generations has been built. The clarity of the exterior wall, and the precision of its painting, are in contrast to the mysterious gloom of the hallowed precinct where the statue of Hercules and the sacred tree are silhouetted against a stormy sky. The wind blowing away the leaves, and the patches of light and dark in the clouds, heighten the atmosphere, and we can understand the awe of the kneeling worshippers and their belief in the elemental power of the gods. The soldier on the left, dramatically standing with his spear on the step as if keeping watch for hidden enemies, has the same profile as the statue and reminds us that the god-hero was venerated by warriors.

PAUL GAUGUIN
Paris 1848 – Dominica, Marquesa Islands 1903
Self-Portrait
Plate 105

Towards the end of the nineteenth century one of those great sea changes, transforming European civilization, was about to take place, not only in art, but in all aspects of human activity. In painting, Impressionism had failed to arrest the increasing bankruptcy of Naturalism. Painters were looking for a new art formula. Gauguin found it in the symbolic use of colour as a means of expressing man's basic emotions and instincts. He spent several years at Pont Aven in Brittany with a group of like-minded artists, and together they developed Synthesism, the pictorial version of the literary Symbolist movement. Synthesism drew its inspiration from various sources: Japanese prints, medieval stained glass and enamels, and for Gauguin a growing interest in primitive art which was to make him reject western civilization and live first in Tahiti, and finally in the South Sea Islands. The self-portrait belongs to his Breton period and was originally a cupboard door in his house. The composition has been reduced to the simplest. It is virtually an abstract pattern of unmodulated red and yellow with some strange yellow flowers in the lower half. Gauguin has shown himself ironically as a saint with a halo, but to counterbalance this there are two apples and a snake, symbols of temptation and evil. The painter's sardonic expression underlines the ambivalence in the portrait, a dichotomy basic to all human nature.

Top Left
105 PAUL GAUGUIN
Self-Portrait
Wood, 79.2 × 51.3 cm
Chester Dale Collection

Left
106 VINCENT VAN GOGH
La Mousmé
Canvas, 73.3 × 60.3 cm
Chester Dale Collection

VINCENT VAN GOGH
Groot Zunder 1853 – Auvers-sur-Oise 1890
La Mousmé
Plate 106

Van Gogh understood the emotional value of colour which, as he said 'gave by its simplification a grander style to things.' He often adopted irrational colours because they were more expressive. This awareness came to him through his knowledge of the Impressionists, whom he met in Paris, and then from living in the sun-charged landscape of southern France. Gauguin visited him there, and although the visit was not a success, it resulted in an even more daring use of flat areas of colour. With this, went an expressive brushwork employing thick impasto where the strokes seem to take on a rhythm of their own. The

girl's name, La Mousmé, is after a character in a Pierre Loti novel, then much in vogue. Her identity is unknown. She is posed in sharp outline against the green background, her hands and face are also in green and are framed by the writhing bentwood chair. Her bodice is painted in vigorous stripes, while the lower part of her skirt with orange dots; the complementary colour of the blue background material is treated as a flat surface. Thus there is a contrast between the head, which is built up through bold brush strokes, and the unmodelled painting of the skirt, another example of van Gogh's debt to Japanese art.

PAUL CÉZANNE
Aix-en-Provence 1939 – 1906
Le Château Noir
Plate 107

Coming from a rich family and not dependent on his paintings for a livelihood, Cézanne was able to ignore the misunderstanding of critics, and patiently and deliberately pursue his researches into painting. The results were of immense importance in the development of modern art. In spite of being closely associated with the Impressionists, he became dissatisfied with their aims, which were concerned only with the visible surface of objects, whereas Cézanne was interested in the underlying structure. Cézanne aimed at eliminating the 'confusions' of emotions and preoccupations everyone carries around with them, by trying to look at everything objectively. He wished to 'paint a living Poussin in the open air, with light and colour', and to bring order into nature by treating it 'by the cylinder, the sphere, the cone, everything in proper perspective so that each side of an object is directed towards a central point.' It

was the repeated search of all classical movements for the monumental and the enduring. Cézanne's landscapes make particular use of his other means to achieve the finality he sought after. Through modulation of colour, he carefully built up a tonal mosaic where each part is in complete harmony with its neighbour and thereby creates an overall unity. Some of his landscapes he painted repeatedly. The Château Noir, actually a farmhouse near Cézanne's home, which he had used as a studio, is the subject of several paintings. It also appears in the many versions of his favourite landscape, Sainte-Victoire. Here, Cézanne has abandoned perspective, as its three-dimensional function conflicts with two-dimensional design. For this reason, the trees and building form a pattern, mainly of verticals and horizontals. The artist has taken liberties with the ruin, making it a four-square medieval keep rather than a simple farmhouse.

CÉZANNE
The Artist's Son, Paul
Plate 108

Paul Cézanne was 13 years old when his father painted his portrait. He sits stolidly, wearing a bowler hat, a common form of headgear for boys of his age, probably rather bored at having to pose. Cézanne demanded great patience from his subjects because he worked slowly and painstakingly, requiring many sittings, and sometimes in the end leaving the portrait unfinished. The incomplete areas in Paul's portrait were the result of Cézanne's determination that every stroke should be exactly right and none

be redundant. This search for perfection went on through his career. At this stage, in 1885, he was still using the Impressionist technique, but the modelling is firmer. This is especially noticeable in the head. In his desire to provide a unifying overall design to the painting, Cézanne has repeated the diagonals of the sloping shoulders and bent arms in the lozenge shapes of the wallpaper. In this way the background takes on the nature of an abstract pattern.

Above
107 PAUL CÉZANNE
Le Château Noir
Canvas, 73.7 × 96.6 cm
Gift of Agnes and Eugene Meyer

Right
108 CÉZANNE
The Artist's Son, Paul
Canvas, 65.3 × 54 cm
Chester Dale Collection

HENRI DE TOULOUSE-LAUTREC
Albi 1864 – Malromé 1901
A Corner of the Moulin de la Galette
Plate 109

Even those with little interest in painting know of the deformed dwarf Toulouse-Lautrec who frequented the brothels, cafés, dance halls and music halls of late nineteenth-century Paris in search of subject matter. Such low-life scenes were rarely represented in art except for their pornographic or scabrous appeal. Lautrec knew this world intimately, inspite of his aristocratic birth, and was able to paint its inhabitants with understanding. He was himself to die from alcoholism. Lautrec saw vice as a fact of life, and he neither made it appear attractive nor condemned it. The people walking about a Paris music hall or having a drink might be expected to enjoy themselves, but they look bored and sad. There is an expressive poignancy in the faces of the two women in the centre. Every face seems to stand out on its own, independently of the others, two seen in sharp profile, and the outlines drawn in black. Such clarity in the composition is a reminder of Lautrec's brilliant posters. He was a masterly draughtsman who could give all the meaning he wanted in a few sure strokes. Gouache allowed him to paint very fluently, carrying over the speed of his drawing, and a similar technique has been applied in this oil by using a very thin medium. All the figures have been kept to the foreground and one has had his head cut off by the top. This gives a feeling of immediacy, and, with the low viewing point, makes us feel part of the crowd.

HENRI ROUSSEAU
Laval 1844 – Paris 1910
The Equatorial Jungle
Plate 110

Interest in primitive and folk art is another aspect of the late nineteenth century's turning away from the classical and Renaissance traditions of western painting. Rousseau was a customs official by profession, and painted in his spare time. He claimed he had visited Mexico during the French intervention, but it is more likely that his exotic landscapes are the result of his imagination reinforced by visits to the Jardin des Plantes, the botanic gardens in Paris. It is customary to call Rousseau naïf, but that does not mean he was simple minded. He was certainly shrewd enough to use his supposed innocence as a means of furthering his art. Rousseau's paintings are not put together haphazardly. The different textures of the fantastic plants in his jungle are juxtaposed to make an interesting pattern, and they help to build up the magical atmosphere which we come to believe in as representing something factual rather than being the result of the artist's vision. A lion and a lioness peer out through the leaves, but they are like the animals in a child's painting. They are intended to be ferocious and yet have an almost friendly expression.

LINTON PARK
1826 – 1906
The Scutching Bee
Plate 111

In America a school of genuine naïf painters grew up in the eighteenth and nineteenth centuries, who, unlike Rousseau, never had the opportunity to come into direct contact with traditional European art. Painting schools and museums were confined to the coastal regions and large towns. Elsewhere in the vast continent, a would-be painter had to draw for his inspiration on popular prints, magazine illustrations or whatever came his way. Dependent on their own imagination, these primitive painters often created works of real power because of the single-mindedness of their vision. They also took everyday scenes as the basis for their compositions and these are of interest to us now because of the picture they give of contemporary life. Park was an eccentric furniture maker and sign painter who also invented a number of useful gadgets. In this incident from life in rural Pennsylvania, a community has banded together in a scutching bee to work the flax. The scutches are also being used in horseplay as a result of the eating and drinking that has taken place beforehand, and these isolated incidents break up the long line of figures and give animation and variety to the picture. The men and women look unusually well dressed for such an occasion, but these communal activities took on a festive character and Park may have wanted to give more colour to the painting by putting his country people into their Sunday best, rather than their drab everyday clothes.

109 HENRI DE TOULOUSE-LAUTREC
A Corner of the Moulin de la Galette
Cardboard on wood, 100.3 × 89.1 cm
Chester Dale Collection

Left
110 HENRI ROUSSEAU
The Equatorial Jungle
Canvas, 140.6 × 129.5 cm
Chester Dale Collection

Below
111 LINTON PARK
The Scutching Bee
Wood, 79.4 × 127.7 cm
Gift of Edgar William and Bernice Chrysler Garbisch

112 WINSLOW HOMER
Right and Left
Canvas, 71.8 × 123 cm
Gift of the Avalon Foundation

WINSLOW HOMER
Boston, Massachusetts 1836 – Scarboro, Maine 1910
Right and Left
Plate 112

Paris and London were still strong attractions for American painters in the period after the Civil War; both Whistler and Sargent settled in Europe. Homer visited France, but his painting remained more consciously American than that of the expatriates. One thing he did bring back with him was an admiration for Manet, and he introduced Impressionist colour and light into his pictures. The settings are generally out of doors, depicting in a factual way, everyday life in the country or by the sea. His subjects have a robust, even aggressive, masculinity about them and are frequently concerned with sailing or shooting. Homer had been a magazine illustrator and this gave an objectiveness and a sense of *rapportage* to his paintings. Nonetheless, he composed his paintings with great artistry; the horizontal lines of the waves and the clouds, providing an almost abstract background, show the influence of Japanese woodcuts. The two ducks have been carefully positioned to form a balanced surface pattern, one plunging into the sea, the other seemingly about to fly out of the canvas in a desperate attempt to escape.

GEORGE BELLOWS
Columbus, Ohio 1882 – New York 1925
Both Members of This Club
Plate 113

Bellows became a pupil of Robert Henri, one of the Ash-can school, who painted the low life of New York at the beginning of this century. Although he sympathized with this group and also painted New York subjects, Bellows was not formally a member. He had been a professional basketball player and followed the athletic world with more interest and knowledge than most painters. He frequented Tom Sharkey's club where professional fights took place, so he painted the boxing match from personal experience. The title is ironical because prize fighting had been made illegal, but the managers kept within the

Above
113 GEORGE BELLOWS
Both Members of This Club
Canvas, 115 × 160.5 cm
Chester Dale Collection

Right
114 EDOUARD VUILLARD
Théodore Duret
Cardboard mounted on wood, 95.2 × 74.8 cm
Chester Dale Collection

law by forming clubs where matches could be fought between supposed members. The brutality of the fight is brought out in the bloody face of the boxer on the left who is slowly sinking to his knees. The two boxers are urged on by the spectators eager for the kill, their faces transformed into twisted masks of cruelty. It is a scene of human degradation worthy of Goya, and the painting has something of his free handling which Bellows had.come to admire as a student. The violence of the subject caused quite a stir when the painting was exhibited and helped to establish the artist's reputation.

EDOUARD VUILLARD
Cuiseaux 1868 – La Baule 1940
Théodore Duret
Plate 114

At first glance this portrait of a writer in his study may seem fairly straightforward, but closer examination shows Vuillard's subtle resolution of compositional and spatial problems. Duret is at the centre of a diamond shape surrounded by two sides of his desk and the two back walls. A pile of books on the right, painted with wonderful freedom, seems about to topple over. This blocks out the fireplace and so brings our eye back to the centre. To prevent any feeling of constriction in the room, the mirror above the chimney-piece reflects the walls we cannot see, thereby amplifying the space. The full-length portrait, visible in the reflection, is one of Duret painted as a younger man by Whistler and now in the Metropolitan Museum, New York. It must have been a poignant reminder to the elderly Duret, sitting with his cat Loulou on his knee, of the past, when as an art critic he had befriended Manet and praised the Impressionists at a time when they needed support.

PIERRE BONNARD
Fontenay-aux-Roses 1867 – Le Cannet 1947
The Letter
Plate 115

Bonnard is probably better represented in America than anywhere else. His simple, happy nature comes out in his paintings and may explain why he is popular with collectors. The vibrant colours he adopted, particularly in his later works, are also immediately appealing. Bonnard is generally linked with Vuillard, and this association is perfectly understandable because the two were close friends and shared a studio. Their styles in these years are similar although both went on to produce distinctive work. In his young days Bonnard was attracted to the circle of writers working for the literary magazine *Revue Blanche,* owned by the Natanson brothers. This painting once belonged to

Alexandre Natanson. The young girl is brought forward almost to the front of the picture plane and seems to be leaning out towards the spectator. The inimate relationship between subject and viewer derives from Japanese prints which also suggested the flattening of the background to a mosaic of decorative shapes. Bonnard's bold use of colour, the patch of blue making up the girl's dress and the warm red of the chair acting as a foil to it, are the result of Gauguin's visits to the artist's studio.

PABLO PICASSO
Malaga 1881 – Mougins 1973
Family of Saltimbanques
Plate 116

Just before he painted this family of circus performers in 1905, Picasso had settled permanently in Paris. The preceding years had not been easy, but now he plunged into the varied social activity that left-bank Paris had to offer. Among the groups he met were clowns and acrobats, whose free and easy life intrigued him as they appeared to lead an existence quite independent of those around them. They form the theme of several paintings, and before starting on his large composition Picasso made preparatory sketches of the individual figures. The subject is enigmatic; no one appears to communicate with anyone else and we do not know what the relationship between the individuals is. The

atmosphere is still and silent, with a touch of sadness, quite unlike the gaiety normally associated with the circus. One is reminded of Velázquez's sad-faced dwarfs, also expected to amuse at the whim of others. Sitting apart, lost in thought, is the young woman. Picasso's change of mind about her hat is clearly visible in a *pentimento*. It has been suggested that the Harlequin on the left is a self-portrait. The principal colour is fawn, and the blues, reds and violets are muted to harmonize in tone.

115 PIERRE BONNARD
The Letter
Canvas, 55 × 47.5 cm
Chester Dale Collection

129

116 PABLO PICASSO
Family of Saltimbanques
Canvas, 212.8 × 229.6 cm
Chester Dale Collection

PICASSO
Nude Woman
Plate 117

In an age of constant and bewildering developments in painting, no artist has been so influential or changed its course more than Picasso. This painting is a key work in Picasso's Analytical Cubist period when he was searching for a style which would convey the volume and mass of an object within the limitations of two-dimensional painting. The solution involved giving several views at once, even if that is something the eye cannot see in real life. *Nude Woman* was painted in 1910 in a Spanish seaside village where Picasso and his mistress, Fernande Olivier, were spending the summer. A series of preliminary drawings enables us to follow his thought as he transformed an intelligible rounded form into almost total abstraction. Analytical Cubism has been compared to the removal of scaffolding around an object revealing the essential structure beneath. The original form has been broken down to its basic components and then reassembled to express the idea of the nude, incorporating different views of her in the same composition. In reaction to the bright colours of the Fauves under Matisse, Picasso uses only greys and browns, and this reinforces the intellectual, rather than the emotional, aspect of the painting.

AMEDEO MODIGLIANI
Leghorn 1884 – Paris 1920
Gypsy Woman with Baby
Plate 118

There were many competent painters in nineteenth-century
Italy, but none made original contributions to European art.
With Modigliani, Italy once more produced an artist of
international calibre. He worked mainly in Paris and led a life
that might have been specially created for a Hollywood film on
la vie de Bohème: drink, drugs and an early death followed by the
suicide of his mistress. Various influences came together in the
formation of Modigliani's very distinctive style. Like so many of
his generation, Cézanne was a powerful influence in the careful
arrangement of colours and the firm outlines of his figures. The
Rumanian sculptor Brancusi, with emphasis on pure form in his
abstract shapes, influenced Modigliani's sense of design. The
features of the gypsy's face, the elongated and almond-shaped
eyes, certainly owe much to an interest in African tribal art,
which also attracted Picasso. Modigliani's study of Italian
painting made him a fine draughtsman, as we can note in the
barest sketching of the woman's form. Her elongated neck goes
back to Botticelli or the sixteenth-century Mannerists whom
Modigliani knew well. The painting belongs to the year before
the artist's death and the theme of a mother and child is probably
a reflection of the recent birth of a daughter to his mistress.

Right
117 PICASSO
Nude Woman
Canvas, 187.3 × 61 cm
Ailsa Mellon Bruce Fund

118 AMEDEO MODIGLIANI
Gypsy Woman with Baby
Canvas, 115.9 × 75 cm
Chester Dale Collection

119 HENRI MATISSE
La Négresse
Paper on canvas (collages), 448 × 670 cm
Ailsa Mellon Bruce Fund

HENRI MATISSE
Le Cateau-Cambrésis 1869 – Vence 1954
La Négresse
Plate 119

In his last 20 years, Matisse increasingly turned to cut-outs or collages, not simply as aids to composition, but as his principal means of expression. It is not surprising that a painter who had always exploited the emotional force of colour should have been attracted to the simple bold shapes of solid colour, often juxtaposed with white. But colour alone was not sufficient. As Matisse, always very conscious of the decorative element in composition, said himself: 'It is not enough to put colours against one another, however beautiful; the colours have to react to one another'. In other words, line and the space around the shapes are equally important. Dissatisfied with what was available commercially, he produced his own painted papers. Using his scissors as a draughtsman would use a pencil, Matisse could achieve the greatest spontaneity by cutting out shapes, often at random, which he would later arrange into a finished work. The figure of *La Négresse* was inspired by the American entertainer Josephine Baker who caused such a sensation in Paris in the 1920s. Matisse has wittily used similar shapes for her legs and arms as for the birds, but they assume a different meaning depending on their position in the painting. The black of the dancing figure and the birds contrasts with the brightly coloured flowers as from a tropical jungle, and all are vividly set against a white background. Matisse believed that art should enhance the joy in life, and his pleasure in creating his cut-outs is communicated in this dazzling composition.

133

120 JACKSON POLLOCK
Lavender Mist
Canvas, 222 × 297.5 cm
Ailsa Mellon Bruce Fund

JACKSON POLLOCK
Cody, Wyoming 1912 – East Hampton, New York 1956
Lavender Mist
Plate 120

With the twentieth century the United States assumed a leading position in the world, not only politically, but also in art. New York replaced Paris as the centre of painting and sculpture, and many non-Americans were attracted there or came as refugees. Among these were many leading Surrealists and they gave Pollock the example of making chance and accident the main principle of creation. His aim was to create 'concrete pictorial sensations', that is, to avoid the memory images which everybody carries about with them and to replace them with sensational images derived from the unconscious. This came to be known as action painting. Pollock used many unorthodox means of applying the paint to his canvases, but the object was always the same, to become integrated with the painting. Pollock explained this himself: 'When I am in my painting, I'm not aware of what I'm doing . . . I have no fears about making changes . . . because the painting has a life of its own. I try to let it come through'. *Lavender Mist* is regarded as one of Pollock's major works.

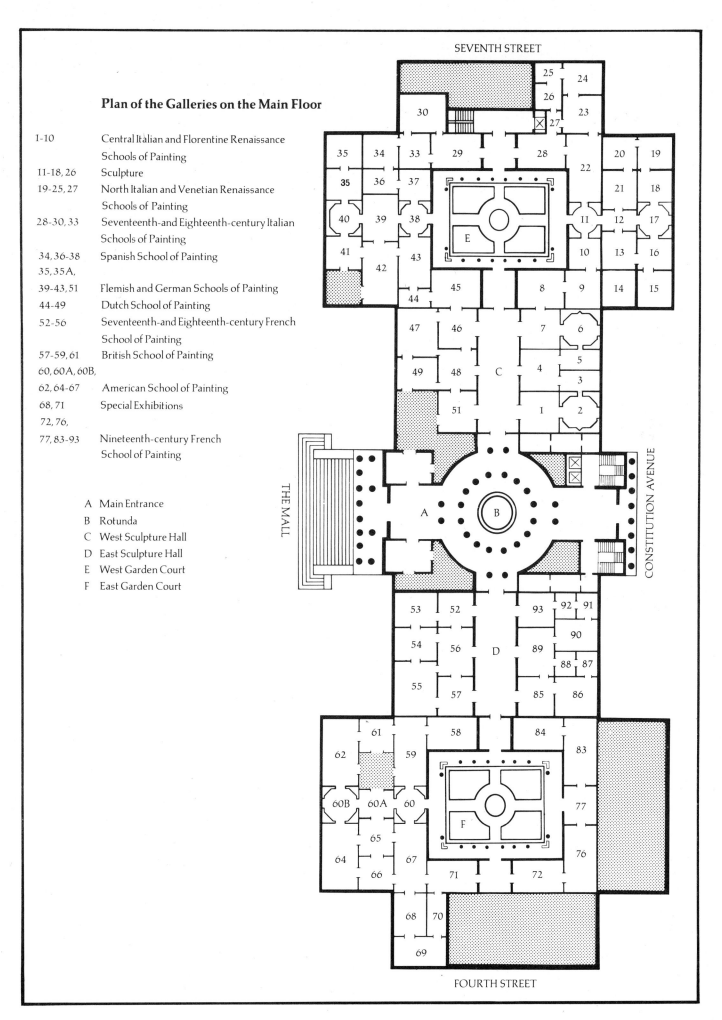

Plan of the Galleries on the Main Floor

1-10	Central Italian and Florentine Renaissance Schools of Painting
11-18, 26	Sculpture
19-25, 27	North Italian and Venetian Renaissance Schools of Painting
28-30, 33	Seventeenth-and Eighteenth-century Italian Schools of Painting
34, 36-38	Spanish School of Painting
35, 35A, 39-43, 51	Flemish and German Schools of Painting
44-49	Dutch School of Painting
52-56	Seventeenth-and Eighteenth-century French School of Painting
57-59, 61	British School of Painting
60, 60A, 60B, 62, 64-67	American School of Painting
68, 71 72, 76,	Special Exhibitions
77, 83-93	Nineteenth-century French School of Painting

A	Main Entrance
B	Rotunda
C	West Sculpture Hall
D	East Sculpture Hall
E	West Garden Court
F	East Garden Court

SEVENTH STREET

FOURTH STREET

THE MALL

CONSTITUTION AVENUE

Index

Page numbers printed in italic type refer to illustrations.